THE WRITE STUFF

A Rib-Tickling Guide to Self-Publishing Stardom

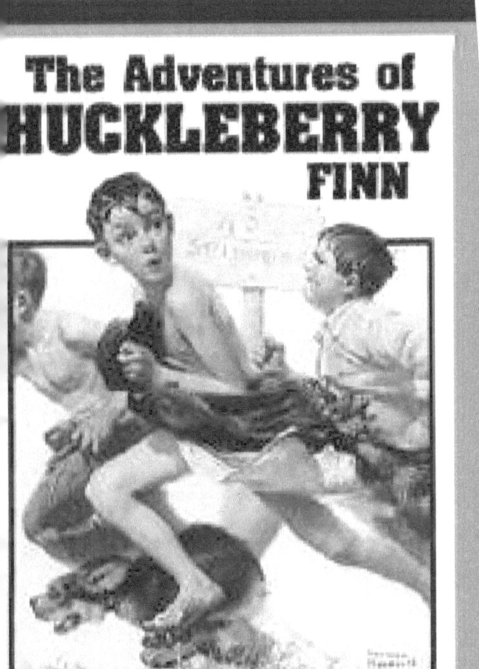

AB MENESES

As always, this book is dedicated to my ever supportive and loving wife,

Maridel

and

our two treasures,

David

and

Gwyneth

Thank you for always supporting all my elusive dreams and schemes.

Introduction

So you want to publish your own book! Alright, let's dive a little deeper into how you can make your book publishing journey cooler and easier. We're not talking about your typical run-of-the-mill "How To" book here. Nope, we're spicing things up with our unique blend of hands-on experience to make this a truly enjoyable ride!

First things first, let's talk about the dreaded budget. We get it, not everyone has a huge bankroll to fund their publishing dreams. But fear not, because we've got some killer tips on how to publish your book without breaking the bank. We've been there, done that, and learned some hard lessons along the way.

Let us guide you through various ways to effectively sell your books online. We'll start by exploring options like online stores and shopping carts, as well as introducing you to our unique workaround system. We'll also show you the advantages of using a money wallet for online selling. Plus, we're throwing in some valuable tips on how to craft an engaging story line for your book. Even if you already have your book ready, you might find our insights helpful. Additionally, we'll recommend the best apps to use in your book-selling journey. You could say this book covers everything you need to know about writing and selling your book. However, the real gem of this book is our workaround system, and if you're eager to dive right into it, simply jump into The Lazy Author's Guide to Online Selling: How to Let Robots Do the Work.

One of the easiest ways to get your book out there is by leveraging online stores. These nifty platforms allow you to upload and sell your book for free. Yep, you heard that right - no up-front costs! Of course, there's a catch - they take a cut from every book you sell. But hey, it's a small price to pay for the convenience of having your book hosted and promoted by a trusted online store. Plus, it's a great option for beginners who are just dipping their toes into the publishing world.

Alright, we get it. You're not just any ordinary author, right? You want to stand out from the crowd and have your own unique online presence. Well, buckle up, because here's where the real fun begins. We'll show you how to sell your book like a pro. Sure, it might sound daunting, but we promise it's not as complicated as it seems.

Now, here's where things get interesting. Online shopping carts are the backbone of any e-commerce website, and they're essential for automating the selling process. But guess what? They can be pricey. Most shopping carts charge you a monthly fee based on the number of items in your cart, whether you make sales or not. Yikes! But don't worry, we've got a sneaky little workaround for you.

This is the gist of this book. We've found a workaround for you to be able to sell your books in your own website, without the monthly payments and all. Sounds interesting? You bet! It's like having the best of two worlds. Sell on online stores for wider coverage and at the same time, sell in your own site without porking out heavy bucks.

You can start small and keep it simple by using our workaround option. Sure, there might be some security risks, but let's be real - everything online comes with a little bit of risk.

Our method is perfect for testing the waters, trying out different strategies, and getting a feel for the market without investing a ton of money up-front. After all, it's all about that proof of concept, right?

Now, let's talk about the elephant in the room - perfectionism. We know it's tempting to obsess over every little detail and make everything perfect before launching your book. But trust us, done is better than perfect. Don't let the fear of imperfection hold you back from getting your book out into the world. Sometimes, taking action and making sales is more important than having everything polished from the get-go.

If you're planning to go big and sell loads of products, then investing in a fancy shopping cart or e-commerce system might be worth it. But if you're just starting out or experimenting with different ideas, why not keep it fun and budget-friendly?

So, why not take a leap of faith, keep it fun and exciting, and start selling your book online? After all, who knows where this adventure might take you? And hey, while you're at it, come check out our online MADGic4U store and see how we've put our own tips into practice. You might even find something you love and want to buy too! Astalavista, amigos! Let's make this publishing journey a wild and memorable ride!

ABMENESES

Table of Contents

From Blank Page to Bestseller

1. **#Hashtag it:** Pick a catchy title that's Insta-worthy and will make your book stand out in the endless sea of social media feeds. *#BookGoals #WritersMasterpiece*

   When it comes to picking a title for your book, go big or go home, amirite? Think outside the box and make sure it's hashtag-worthy! Choose something that'll make readers stop scrolling through their feeds and be like, "Whoa, I need to check out that book ASAP!" #BookGoals all the way! Or better yet, create a title that screams "Writers Masterpiece" and watch your book rise to Insta-stardom! It's all about that click-worthy title game! *#TitleGameStrong #AuthorsRockinIt*

2. **No Filter:** Don't be afraid to write what you really feel. Be authentic and relatable, just like your favorite filter-free influencer. Keep it real!

   No filter, no problem! When it comes to writing your book, forget about sugar-coating or holding back. Readers love authenticity, just like their favorite influencers who spill the tea without any fancy filters. So, let those words flow, keep it real, and let your readers know you're not here to play games. After all, who needs filters when you've got that raw, unfiltered vibe? You got this, fam! *#NoFilterWriting #AuthenticAF*

3. **Emojis are Lit:** Sprinkle some emojis in your writing to add that extra level of emotion. Because nothing says "I'm feeling it" like a 😂 or a 😍. Am I right?

   Emojis are like the glitter of the digital world, and they're lit AF! When you're writing your book, why not spice things up with a sprinkle of those cute little pictograms? They're like tiny emotion bombs that explode with feelings! 😂 for hilarious moments, 😍 for heart-fluttering romance, or 🤯 for mind-blowing plot twists! Emojis are the perfect way to add that extra level of emotion to your words, and let your readers know you're not here to be basic. Because let's be real, nothing says "I'm feeling it" like a well-placed emoji! So go ahead, express yourself with those tiny, colorful icons and watch your book shine with flair! 🚀 📚 💥 *#EmojisAreLife #FeelingIt #AuthorsRockingEmojis*

4. **Binge-Writing:** Procrastination is so yesterday. Set aside some serious binge-writing time, just like you do for your favorite Netflix series. Grab your laptop, a bag of avocado chips, and go all in!

Forget procrastination, it's so last season! When it's time to write your book, it's all about that binge-writing life, just like how you binge-watch your favorite Netflix series. Set aside some serious *"do not disturb"* time, grab your laptop, put on your cozy socks, and get ready to slay that keyboard like a boss!

And hey, just like how you snack on avocado chips while watching your shows, stock up on those approved snacks to keep you fueled during your writing marathon. Think kombucha, matcha lattes, or acai bowls - whatever gets your creative juices flowing! Who says writing can't be as enjoyable as your guilty-pleasure TV time?

So, go all in and binge-write like a champ! Say goodbye to the dreaded "I'll do it later" mentality and hello to some serious writing hustle. You got this, wordsmith! 🚀 📝 🫐 *#BingeWritingMode #AvocadoChipFuel #AuthorsWritingMarathon*

5. **Meme Magic:** Inject some meme magic into your writing. Readers love a good laugh, so why not drop a "distracted boyfriend" or a "dank meme" reference? LOL!

   Readers and memes go together like avocado and toast, so why not sprinkle some meme magic into your writing? Injecting a well-timed "distracted boyfriend" or a "dank meme" reference can add that extra spice to your book that readers crave!

   Imagine your readers snorting with laughter as they come across a clever meme reference in your writing. It's like a secret handshake that instantly bonds you with your fellow readerss. LOL! Whether it's a witty pop culture reference or a relatable meme moment, it's all about bringing on those giggles and making your readers go "Yaaasss!"

   So, don't be afraid to tap into the meme culture and unleash some meme magic in your writing. Embrace the power of the meme, and watch your book become an internet sensation! 📚 🥥 😂 *#MemeMagic #MillennialLaughs #DistractedBoyfriendWorthy*

6. **Coffee is Life:** Caffeinate thyself! Coffee is the fuel that powers millennial creativity. So, grab your latte, put on your oversized glasses, and let the words flow!

Coffee is the elixir of life, the potion that fuels creativity! It's the secret weapon that powers our writing sessions and keeps us going like a boss. So, channel your inner coffee connoisseur, grab that latte with extra foam, slip on those oversized glasses, and let the caffeine do its magic!

Just like how latte art is a masterpiece, let your words flow and create your own literary masterpiece. With every sip, feel the ideas percolate in your brain and the words come to life on the page. It's like a caffeinated symphony of creativity!

And hey, if you need a refill, don't hesitate to indulge in a little *"coffee break"* time. After all, a well-timed coffee break can do wonders for your writing flow. So, embrace the coffee culture, caffeinate thyself, and let the world be amazed by the literary genius that's brewing inside you! *#CoffeeIsLife #FuelForCreativity #LatteArtOfWriting*

7. **Diverse AF:** Representation matters! Make sure your characters are as diverse as your group chat. It's time to break stereotypes and celebrate inclusivity in your writing.

Representation is lit! Just like how your group chat is a diverse squad with different backgrounds, beliefs, and emoji preferences, your book characters should be just as diverse AF! It's time to break those tired old stereotypes and celebrate inclusivity in your writing.

No more cookie-cutter characters or one-dimensional cliches. Mix it up, yo! Embrace characters of all genders, races, sexual orientations, religions, and abilities. Let your story reflect the beautiful tapestry of humanity, and let your readers see themselves in your characters.

Remember, representation matters! Your writing has the power to create a world where everyone feels seen and heard. So, go ahead and challenge the status quo, shatter those glass ceilings, and create characters that are as unique and diverse as your lit group chat. It's time to write a new chapter of inclusivity in your book! 📚 🦾 💪 *#DiverseAF #RepresentationMatters #InclusiveWritingVibes*

8. **Keep it Short and Snappy:** Attention spans are shorter than a Snapchat story, so keep your chapters short and snappy. Readers love a quick read between their busy work and social media schedule.

Ain't nobody got time for long chapters! Readers are living in the fast lane with busy work schedules, social media scrolling, and TikTok binging. So, keep your writing short and snappy, like a Snapchat story that disappears in a flash!

Think bite-sized chapters that can be devoured during a quick coffee break or a subway commute. Keep the pace brisk and the dialogue witty, and watch your readers get hooked faster than a viral tweet! Readers love a quick read that fits seamlessly into their on-the-go lifestyle.

And hey, don't forget to sprinkle in some emoji action to add that extra level of expressiveness. Because who needs lengthy descriptions when you can just use a 😂 or a 🙅‍♀️, am I right? Keep it short, keep it snappy, and watch your book become the go-to read for readers on the move! 📚✍️💬 *#ShortAndSnappy* *#MillennialReads* *#EmojiExpressiveness*

9. **Beta Buds:** Find your beta buds - fellow readerss who will read and critique your work with brutal honesty. They'll be your ride-or-die squad on this writing journey.

Yo, find your ride-or-die squad for that beta reading game! Your fellow readers can be your ultimate beta buds who read your work and give you that brutally honest feedback you need. They'll be your crew to ride through the highs and lows of this writing journey!

Look for those who will give you the real deal, no sugar-coating allowed. They'll spot plot holes faster than they swipe left on a dating app and catch grammar mistakes quicker than autocorrect. Their feedback will be as lit as a viral tweet!

But remember, it's a two-way street. Be ready to return the favor and critique their work with the same level of savage honesty. It's all about helping each other level up and create the best darn book possible.

So, gather your beta buds, create a group chat, and brace yourself for some serious critique sessions mixed with emoji reactions and meme-worthy feedback. Your ride-or-die squad will be there to celebrate your wins, console you through the rejections, and keep you motivated

to slay that writing game! 📚🔥🎬💀 *#BetaBuds*
#HonestCritiques #WritingSquadGoals

10. **Self-Care Breaks:** Remember to take self-care breaks, because burnt-out writers are not cute. Stretch, do some downward dogs, or binge-watch a season of your favorite show. You deserve it!

    Listen up! Self-care is key in this writing hustle. Don't let yourself burn out like a stale meme. Take those self-care breaks like a boss!

    Stretch those fingers and do some downward dogs to avoid writer's cramp. Your body needs some TLC, just like your manuscript. And speaking of TLC, binge-watching a season of your favorite show can be the ultimate self-care treat. So, grab that remote, cuddle up with your favorite blanket, and indulge in some guilty pleasure TV time.

    Remember, burnt-out writers are not cute. You deserve to take care of yourself like the fabulous wordsmith you are. Treat yourself with love and kindness, and come back to your writing with a refreshed mind and body.

    And hey, don't forget to share some Insta-worthy pics of your self-care breaks with your writing buddies. They'll appreciate the self-care inspo and might even join you in a virtual yoga session or a TV show marathon. Keep it chill, keep it fun, and keep that self-care game strong! 🧘💀📺🍿
    #SelfCareBreaks #WriterWellness #TreatYoSelf

There you have it, tips to help you write your own book the right way. Now, go forth and slay that keyboard like the literary boss that you are! You got this, fam! 💪📚✨

How To Get Those Creative Juices Flowing

If you're looking to slay the writing game and make your story go viral, check out these story ideas that are totally on-trend right now. From magical creatures to dystopian adventures, these are the stories that are *#goals for today's readers.*

The **"Insta-Worthy Magical Creatures"**: Imagine a world where unicorns are the new influencers, and mermaids run their own underwater beauty salon. It's a fantastical realm where hashtags and spells collide, and the magic is as vibrant as an Instagram filter.

The **"Tech Gone Wild"**: Picture a future where emojis come to life, and social media platforms have taken over the world. From rogue hashtags to virtual reality gone haywire, it's a sci-fi thriller with a digital twist that will have readers hooked till the last page.

The **"Foodie Quest"**: Join a group of culinary adventurers on a quest for the ultimate recipe that can cure any ailment. From a ramen master with a secret ingredient to a cupcake wizard with a hidden recipe book, it's a gastronomic journey that will make readers' taste buds tingle.

The **"Time-Traveling TikTokers"**: When a group of Gen Z time travelers accidentally gets stuck in the past, they must navigate history's greatest moments while trying to keep their viral TikTok account a secret. It's a hilarious and nostalgic adventure that will have readers LOL-ing all the way through.

The **"Superhero Sidekicks"**: Move over, superheroes! It's time for the sidekicks to shine. Follow a misfit crew of sidekicks as they team up to save the world from a supervillain, all while dealing with their own unique set of powers and quirks. It's a humorous and action-packed ride that will make readers root for the underdogs.

The **"Hilarious Haunted House"**: When a group of friends inherits a creepy old mansion, they think they've hit the jackpot - until they realize the house is haunted by a mischievous ghost with a penchant for practical jokes. It's a spooky and sidesplitting tale that will have readers giggling and gasping in equal measure.

The **"Epic Quest for Wi-Fi"**: In a post-apocalyptic world where the internet is long gone, a group of friends embarks on a perilous journey to find the last remaining Wi-Fi hotspot. From battling mutant creatures to navigating treacherous terrains, it's a quest for connection that will resonate with today's digital natives.

The **"Quirky Love Story"**: When two polar opposites meet in the most unexpected way, sparks fly - but not in the usual swoon-worthy romance kind of way. It's a quirky and unconventional love story full of witty banter, awkward encounters, and unexpected twists that will warm readers' hearts and make them LOL.

The **"Eco-Warrior Adventure"**: In a world ravaged by climate change, a group of eco-warriors bands together to protect the last remaining natural resources from a greedy corporation. It's a thrilling and timely tale that will inspire readers to take action and save the planet, one page at a time.

The **"Influencer Gone Rogue"**: Follow the rise and fall of a social media influencer who goes from online fame to offline infamy. From staged photoshoots to fake personas, it's a satirical and hilarious take on the world of influencers that will have readers scrolling through the pages with delight.

So, there you have it, squad - in-demand story ideas that are lit AF and ready to rock the literary world. Choose your favorite, unleash your creative vibes, and let your imagination run wild! These stories are all about capturing the zeitgeist of our times, with a twist of humor and wit that will keep readers coming back for more. So, grab your writing gear, channel your inner wordsmith, and get ready to slay those story goals. Remember, you've got this, and with these ideas, you'll be on your way to being the next big thing in the literary world. Happy writing! *#StoryGoals #LitAF #WordWizardsUnite*

How to Pen a Bestseller in Your Pajamas

Wondering when the stars align for you to embark on your epic book-writing journey? Well, listen up, because we've got the tea on the perfect timing to get that literary masterpiece rolling!

"Post-Breakup Blues": When you're going through a heartbreak, why not turn that emotional rollercoaster into some serious writing fuel? Pour your heart out on the pages, channel those feelings into your characters, and who knows, you might just end up with a breakup bestseller!

"Procrastination Purgatory": We all know that feeling when you're stuck in the never-ending loop of procrastination. Well, why not break free from the cycle and put that idle time to good use? Writing a book can be the ultimate productive escape from the endless scroll of social media and binge-watching.

"Vacation Vibes": Picture yourself lounging on a beach with a fancy drink in hand, soaking up the sun and letting your creative juices flow. Yep, writing a book can be the perfect sidekick to your dream vacation, giving you the chance to unwind and let your imagination run wild.

"Late-Night Insomniac": Can't sleep? Instead of counting sheep, why not count words? If you find yourself tossing and turning in the wee hours of the night, grab your laptop and let your creativity flow freely. Who knows, your sleep-deprived brain might just come up with some genius story ideas!

"New Year, New Book": Looking for a fresh start in the new year? Writing a book can be the ultimate resolution! Set some writing goals, create a writing routine, and make it your mission to bring your story to life in the coming year. It's a creative challenge that's worth taking on!

"Snowed-In Bliss or Rainy Day Snugs": When bad weather hits and you're cozied up at home with a cup of hot cocoa, it's the perfect time to hunker down and get those writing juices flowing. Let the rain or snowstorm outside be your inspiration, and let your creativity flourish in the warmth of your writing nook.

"Career Hiatus": Taking a break from the hustle and bustle of work life? Why not use that downtime to fulfill your writing dreams? Whether you're on sabbatical or taking a gap year, it's a golden opportunity to dedicate some serious time and effort to your book.

"Birthday Bonanza": Another year older and wiser? Writing a book can be the ultimate way to celebrate your birthday! Treat yourself to some writing time, indulge in your creative passions, and make it a memorable birthday gift to yourself.

"Boring Commute": If you find yourself stuck in a never-ending commute, turn that mundane time into a writing adventure! Whip out your notebook or fire up your laptop, and let your imagination take you on a journey while you're on the road or on public transport. It's a creative way to make the most out of a boring situation.

"Right Here, Right Now": The truth is, there's no perfect time to write a book. The best time is NOW! Don't wait for the stars to align or for the perfect moment to arrive. Just start writing, no matter where you are or what time of year it is. The sooner you start, the closer you'll be to holding your finished book in your hands!

So, there you have it, fellow word wizards - the best times to write a book that are both funny and relatable to our readers. Whether you're going through a breakup, procrastinating, on vacation, snowed in, or just craving some creative time, there's never a wrong time to put pen to paper *(or fingers to keyboard)* and start crafting your literary masterpiece. So, go ahead and seize the moment, chase those writing dreams, and slay those writing goals like the word warriors you are! Remember, the world is waiting to be captivated by your story, and you've got the creative mojo to make it happen. Get those fingers typing, those words flowing, and let your imagination run wild. You've got this, fam! *#WriteNow #WordWarrior #BookGoals*

The Great Font Hunt: A Comical Quest for Bookish Beauty

Picking the right fonts for your reading materials is like choosing the perfect filter for your Insta post - it's gotta be on point! So, here are 14 killer tips for all you digital-savvy, font-freaks out there:

1. **Keep it Legit:** Legibility is key, bros and babes! Ain't nobody got time for squinting at some fancy font that looks like a squished bug. Go for fonts that are easy on the eyes and don't make your readers feel like they need glasses.

2. **Match the Vibe:** Font vibes matter! If you're designing a flyer for a beach party, don't go with a font that looks like it belongs in a corporate report. Keep it groovy and go for fonts that vibe with your overall design.

3. **Mix it Up:** Don't be afraid to mix and match! Pairing different fonts can add some serious flavor to your reading materials. Just make sure they complement each other like PB and J, and not clash like orange juice after brushing your teeth.

4. **Size Matters:** Size it up, folks! Don't go all microscopic on your readers or blow it up like it's the headline of the century. Find that sweet spot where it's easy to read without squinting or feeling like you're reading a billboard.

5. **Know Your Audience:** It's all about the people, peeps! Think about who you're designing for - are they hipsters, gamers, or grandma? Different audiences may have different preferences, so keep that in mind when picking your fonts.

6. **Brand It Up:** Brand it like a boss! If you're designing for a specific brand, make sure your fonts match their vibe. You don't want to give off mixed signals like wearing socks with sandals.

7. **Be Unique:** Stand out, my dudes and dudettes! Don't go for the same old boring fonts that

everyone and their mom uses. Dare to be different and find a font that screams "you"!

8. **Check the Spacing:** Give it some breathing room, peeps! Tight spacing can make your text look like a hot mess. Make sure your letters have some space to breathe and chill.

9. **Test for Readability:** Test it out, squad! Don't just rely on your own eyes, but get feedback from others too. If your BFF can't read your font without squinting, it's time to rethink your choice.

10. **Consider Context:** Context is king! Think about where your reading materials will be used. Is it for a website, a poster, or a social media post? Different contexts may require different fonts, so choose wisely.

11. **Stay on Brand:** Don't go rogue on your brand, peeps! If you're creating materials for a company or organization, make sure your font aligns with their brand guidelines. You don't want to get a stern email from the marketing team.

12. **Avoid Font Overload:** Less is more, squad! Don't go all crazy and use every font you can find in your design. Stick to a few fonts that complement each other and keep it clean and classy.

13. **Consider Accessibility:** Accessibility rocks, my dudes! Not all fonts are created equal when it comes to accessibility. Make sure your font is readable for people with visual impairments, and consider using fonts that are designed with accessibility in mind.

14. **Have Fun:** Don't forget to have a blast, fam! Picking fonts can be a creative adventure, so enjoy the process and let your inner design guru shine!

There you have it, peeps! Follow these tips and you'll be rocking some killer fonts in your reading materials like a pro. Happy designing and may the font gods be ever in your favor! Keep it funky, fresh, and totally lit with fonts that make your readers go "Wow, that's dope!" Now go forth and slay those font choices like the cool cat you are. Peace out! ✌️ 😎🔥

Epic Fails: When Words Go Rogue and Grammar Gets Lost

Everybody gotta start somewhere, right? From Robert Ludlum to John Green, to Christina Lauren, to J.K. Rowling — they all started at the bottom of the barrel, so to speak. And for sure, they've committed some, uhm, embarrassing it may be to admit, some bo-boo along the way. So, don't worry messing up early in your career. It will be your learning experience as you improve on your craft. Haha! I'm sure you'll be laughing at your "writing fail" later in the future saying, "I DID THAT?!!"

Alright, buckle up! We're about to dive into the most epic fails of trying to pen down the next great novel. From cringe-worthy typos to plot holes big enough to drive a semi-truck through, these writing fails are straight-up savage. Let's get this lit train rolling!

The "Too Many Prologues" Fail: You know you're in trouble when your book starts with not one, but three prologues. It's like trying to choose which filter to put on your Instagram story - #overkill!

The "World-Building Gone Wild" Fail: Sure, creating a unique fantasy world is cool, but when you need a PhD in mythology just to understand the lore, you've gone too far. Ain't nobody got time for that!

The "Character Amnesia" Fail: When your protagonist changes eye color halfway through the book, it's like a case of mistaken identity on steroids. Who are you, and what have you done with the main character?

The "Dialogue Disaster" Fail: Writing dialogue that sounds like a Shakespearean play on a bad acid trip? Yeah, that's gonna be a no from us, dawg. Keep it real and relatable, yo!

The "Tropes Galore" Fail: From the damsel in distress to the brooding bad boy with a tragic past, clichéd tropes can make your book feel as stale as week-old avocado toast. Spice it up, peeps!

The "Plot Twist Whiplash" Fail: When your plot twist is so out of left field that readers get literary whiplash, you've officially gone off the rails. Slow your roll and keep it believable, homie!

The "Grammar Grenade" Fail: Poor grammar and typos can turn your writing into a hot mess faster than a Snapchat streak gone wrong. Proofread, people - it's not rocket science!

The "Info Dump Overload" Fail: We get it, you did your research, but bombarding readers with a textbook worth of info dumps is a surefire way to put them to sleep faster than a meditation app.

The "TMI Tornado" Fail: Describing every single mundane detail, from the color of the walls to the protagonist's sock preference, is a surefire way to lose readers faster than you can say "TL;DR."

The "Unbelievable Romance" Fail: Love at first sight, instant soulmates, and fairy tale endings may work in Disney movies, but in a book, it's like a bad Tinder date gone wrong. Keep it real, peeps!

The "Plot Hole Potholes" Fail: Plot holes so big you could drive a semi-truck through them? Yeah, that's a recipe for a literary disaster. Close those gaps like a pro!

The "Overused Adverbs" Fail: Using adverbs excessively can turn your writing into a cringey middle school essay. Show, don't tell, and avoid those -ly words like the plague!

The "Word Salad" Fail: Sentences so convoluted and tangled that readers need a compass and a Sherpa to navigate them? Ain't nobody got time for that linguistic acrobatics!

The "Too Many POV's" Fail: Switching between multiple points of view like a DJ on a caffeine high can leave readers more confused than a dog trying to solve a Rubik's cube. Keep it simple, folks!

The "Too Many Exclamation Points" Fail: Exclamation points are like the seasoning of writing - a little goes a long way. But if your book looks like a text from your overly enthusiastic grandma, with exclamation points after every sentence, it's time to dial it down, sis!

The "Random Plot Twists" Fail: Suddenly revealing that the villain is actually a talking llama from another dimension? Yeah, that's a plot twist that's gonna leave readers scratching their heads like they just walked out of a physics lecture. Keep it coherent, bro!

The "Superfluous Prose" Fail: Going overboard with flowery language and purple prose is like drowning your book in a thesaurus. Readers just want to enjoy the story, not decipher a cryptic crossword puzzle!

The "Lost in Punctuation" Fail: Throwing in commas, semicolons, and dashes like confetti at a party can turn your writing into a grammatical maze. Keep it simple and punctuate with purpose, peeps!

The "Overused Cliches" Fail: From "dark and stormy nights" to "tears streaming down her face like a waterfall," cliches can make your writing feel as stale as day-old bread. Let's retire those tired phrases, please!

The "Unfinished Ending" Fail: Ending your book with a cliffhanger so abrupt it feels like you got cut off mid-sentence is like leaving your readers stranded on a deserted island. Give them some closure, homie!

So, there you have it, folks - the top hilarious fails in writing a book that will leave you in stitches. But hey, we've all been there, and learning from these fails is part of the writing journey. So, keep writing, stay lit, and may the words be ever in your favor! Peace out! ✌️ 📚😂

The Self-Publisher's Survival Kit: Wit, Wisdom and Whimsy

This is it! How to publish a book on your own

Ready to take on the literary world and publish your own masterpiece? Congratulation, but hep, hep, hep, hold your horses. Like it or not, there are some things you need to know to be able to publish your own book successfully. Yup, that's what this book is all about. We'll guide you every step of the way until you are publishing books like a pro.

Okidoki, for starters, here are some basic steps to slay the game and get your book out there like a boss. You don't have to follow everything, just play it by ear. Whatever feels good to you, then go for it.

1. **Dream It, Scream It:** First things first, decide what you want to write about and let your creativity run wild! Get those creative juices flowing and come up with a lit idea for your book. Whether it's a heartwarming romance or an epic sci-fi saga, make sure your book idea has you doing cartwheels with excitement. It could be a quirky rom-com, a thrilling mystery, or an epic fantasy. Whatever floats your bookish boat!

   It's time to unleash your creative beast and dream up a tale that'll make readers swoon, gasp, and maybe even snort with laughter. So, grab your trusty quill or your keyboard of glory, and let's set sail on a literary adventure!

   Think about what gets your heart pumping with excitement. Is it a steamy romance set on a tropical island where the waves crash against the shore as two star-crossed lovers find solace in each other's arms? Or perhaps it's an intergalactic odyssey where aliens with tentacles and three heads battle for the fate of the universe in an epic sci-fi saga?

   Whatever it is, make sure your book idea makes you do cartwheels like a kid on a sugar high. You're the captain of this literary ship, so let your imagination run wild like a herd of wild unicorns on a sugar rush!

And don't be afraid to scream it from the rooftops! Share your book idea with your friends, family, and even the barista at your favorite coffee shop. Let them know that you're about to embark on a writing journey that's going to be as epic as a dragon's hoard of treasure.

Remember, your book idea is the spark that will ignite your writing process. So, let it be as wild and exciting as a roller coaster ride at a theme park. Get ready to buckle up and let your creativity take the wheel as you bring your dream book to life!

So, dream it, scream it, and let your imagination soar. Your readers are eagerly waiting to be whisked away on a literary adventure they won't forget. Happy writing, oh daring author! May your words flow like a river and your creativity shine like a supernova in the literary galaxy!

Alright, squad, it's time to get those creative vibes flowing and come up with an idea that's lit AF for your book! Think outside the box and let your imagination run wild. Maybe you're all about that quirky rom-com that will make readers LOL, or you're itching to write a spine-tingling mystery that will keep them on the edge of their seats. Or hey, why not go all-in with an epic fantasy that transports readers to a whole new world? Whatever floats your bookish boat, fam! Just remember, this is your chance to shine and show off your literary swagger, so don't hold back. Let those idea sparks fly and watch your bookish dreams take flight! *#LitIdeasOnly #BookishImagination #ImaginationOnFire*

2. **Writing Frenzy - Get Your Write On:** Time to whip out your trusty laptop or notebook and go on a writing spree. Channel your inner wordsmith and pour your heart and soul into your story. Pro tip: stock up on coffee and snacks for those writing marathons!

    Time to unleash your writing beast mode and go on a writing frenzy! Grab your trusty laptop or notebook, find your writing nook, and let those words flow like a river. Channel your inner wordsmith and pour your heart and soul into your story. Don't hold back, let your creative juices flow like there's no tomorrow! Pro tip: stock up on coffee, snacks, and all your favorite brain-boosting treats to fuel those writing marathons. We're talking pizza, chocolate, and all the guilty pleasures that keep you going when writer's block comes knocking. So buckle up, fam, it's time to rock that writing game and make your story shine brighter than the sun!

    Yes! It's time to unleash the power of your pen or the fury of your keyboard as you embark on the noble quest of writing your book. Ready to conquer the blank page like a literary ninja? Let's get your write on!

    Grab your trusty pen, your favorite notebook, or fire up your keyboard with the intensity of a rocket launch. Embrace your inner wordsmith and let your creativity flow like a mighty river. Whether you're in your writing nook, at a coffee shop, or even in your PJs in bed, make that writing space your literary command center!

Pour your heart and soul into your manuscript like a master chef adding just the right spices to create a delectable dish. Let your characters come alive, your plot twist and turn like a roller coaster, and your dialogue crackle like a bonfire on a starry night. You're the captain of this literary ship, so let your imagination sail into uncharted waters!

But beware, ye scallywags! The treacherous waters of writer's block and self-doubt may try to thwart your progress. Stay vigilant, and keep pushing forward with the tenacity of a determined pirate hunting for hidden treasure. Remember, the first draft doesn't need to be perfect. Just let your creativity flow freely and let your story take shape.

And don't forget to have fun! Writing is your grand adventure, and you're the hero wielding the power of words. So, throw in a witty one-liner, create quirky characters, and weave in clever references that make you chuckle. After all, if you're not enjoying the journey, who will?

So, hoist the Jolly Roger of your pen or keyboard, and let your story sail towards the horizon of literary greatness! Get your write on, and may your words be as dazzling as a fireworks display on the Fourth of July! *#WritingBeastMode #CreativeJuicesFlowing #SnacksAndWordsmithing*

3. **Editing Dance - Edit Like a Pro:** Once you've got your first draft down, it's time to polish it like a pro. Edit, revise, and repeat until your manuscript is on fleek. . Trim those excess adjectives, squash those pesky typos, and polish your prose until it

shines like a diamond. Don't be afraid to kill your darlings, but watch out for those typos - they can be sneaky little devils! Remember, a well-edited book is a treasure trove for readers!

Alright, squad, it's time to bust out those editing moves and dance your way to a manuscript that's on fleek! Once you've got that first draft down, it's all about the polish game. Edit, revise, and repeat like a pro until your story shines like a diamond. Don't be afraid to slay those darlings that aren't serving the plot, but watch out for those sneaky little devils called typos. They can creep up on you like a ninja! So grab your red pen or fire up that editing software, and get ready to dance your way to manuscript perfection. Let's show those typos who's boss and make that story shine brighter than a disco ball on a Saturday night!

Just like a skilled chef, it's time to trim those excess adjectives that are as plentiful as a buffet at an all-you-can-eat restaurant. Too many adjectives can weigh down your sentences like an anchor, so cut them back and let your words breathe. Remember, it's quality over quantity!

And watch out for those pesky typos that can sneak in like mischievous imps. Hunt them down with the precision of a ninja, armed with your trusty red pen or the "Find" function on your computer. Don't let those little buggers ruin the party for your readers!

Polish your prose until it shines like a diamond in the rough. Smooth out any rough edges, reword clunky sentences, and make sure your dialogue sparkles like a gem. Every word should earn its place in your manuscript, so make sure they're all worthy of the spotlight!

But remember, editing is not about stripping away your unique voice or style. It's about bringing out the best in your words and making them shine even brighter. Think of it as giving your manuscript a spa day, where it comes out looking refreshed, rejuvenated, and ready to conquer the literary world!

So, grab your editor's hat, put on your keen eye, and edit like a pro. Your readers will thank you for it, and your book will be a treasure trove of literary excellence that'll leave them begging for more! Arrr, matey, ye be a wordsmith extraordinaire!

#EditingMoves #ManuscriptOnFleek #TyposBeware

4. **Eye-Catching Cover Slay:** They say don't judge a book by its cover, but let's be real, we all do. Design a killer cover that captures the essence of your book and makes it stand out on the shelves *(or virtual shelves, in this digital age).* Pish posh! Your book cover is the siren song that lures readers in. So, create a captivating cover that screams "Pick me up!" and watch your book fly off the shelves *(or virtual shelves).*

   Alright, peeps, listen up! It's time to talk about "Cover Slay," aka the art of making your book cover game strong. They say "don't judge a book by its cover," but let's be honest, we all do it anyway. Don't let anyone tell ye not to judge a book by its cover, for that's just a load of bilge water! Your book cover be the siren song that beckons readers from afar, and ye best make sure it's as captivating as a treasure map leading to buried literary loot! So, if you're an aspiring author ready to drop a literary bomb, buckle up and let's get into it!

First things first, your book cover has got to be on fleek. It's like the outfit you wear to a party - it's gotta slay and make heads turn. Think bold, eye-catching, and totally Instagrammable. You want that cover to be the queen bee of the bookshelf or the virtual shelves, depending on your vibe.

But it's not just about looking pretty, y'all. Your cover has to capture the essence of your book. It's like a Tinder profile pic - it's gotta give potential readers a sneak peek into what they're gonna get. Is your book funny? Mysterious? Romantic? Sci-fi? Make sure your cover says it loud and clear, so readers know what they're signing up for.

And let's talk about standing out in this digital age. We're talking about virtual shelves, baby! With so many books available online, your cover has to be a total showstopper. Think bold colors, unique fonts, and killer graphics that make people want to click that "Add to Cart" button faster than they can say "Amazon Prime."

And don't forget about your target audience. Your cover has to speak their language. If you're writing a book, it better have that vibe that speaks to your readers. If you're targeting romance readers, make sure it's giving off all those heart eyes emoji vibes. Know your audience and slay that cover game accordingly.

So, there you have it. Cover Slay is all about making your book cover pop, capturing your book's essence, standing out in the digital jungle, and speaking to your target audience. Get those creative juices flowing, and let's see you rock that book cover like a boss!

Think of yer book cover as the grand entrance to a swanky literary ball. It's the first thing readers see, and it better make 'em want to grab that book and dive in faster than a pirate after a chest of gold. So, let your creativity run wild and create a cover that screams "Pick me up!" like a parrot on a shoulder.

Consider the colors, the fonts, and the imagery that'll make yer book cover stand out like a shiny doubloon among a sea of books. Make it eye-catching, intriguing, and utterly irresistible. After all, a book cover that doesn't turn heads is like a ship without a sail, drifting aimlessly in the literary ocean.

Whether yer book be in print or digital, yer cover should be as alluring as a siren's call. It should make readers want to reach out and grab it, as if they're about to embark on a thrilling adventure or uncover a hidden treasure. So, hoist the Jolly Roger of your creativity and create a book cover that'll make waves and send yer book flying off the shelves *(or virtual shelves)* like a cannonball!

Remember, a captivating book cover be the key to unlocking the hearts and minds of readers. So, polish yer cover until it shines like a gem and let it be the beacon that guides readers to yer literary treasure. Arrr, me hearties, with a captivating cover, yer book be sure to make a splash in the vast ocean of books!

5. **Publishing Hustle:** Time to decide how you want to publish your book. Traditional publishing? Self-publishing? Hybrid publishing? Do your research and choose the path that works best for you and your bookish dreams. Team Up with Pros: Self-publishing doesn't mean you have to go it alone. Consider hiring professionals like editors, proofreaders, and cover designers to give your book that extra shine. They're the wind in your authorial sails!

When it comes to self-publishing, remember, you don't have to ride the literary waves all by yourself. It's time to assemble your own literary Avengers and team up with the pros to make your book shine brighter than the Vegas strip!

Just like a baseball team needs a pitcher to throw fastballs and a catcher to nab those foul balls, your book needs a team of professionals to bring out its full potential. Consider hiring editors, proofreaders, and cover designers to be the wind in your authorial sails!

Editors are like the coaches of your literary team. They'll help you refine your story, smooth out the rough spots, and make sure your words hit the right notes. They'll be your guiding star, helping you navigate the treacherous waters of grammar, punctuation, and plot twists.

Proofreaders are the MVPs of the editing game. They'll catch those sneaky typos, grammar gaffes, and punctuation blunders that can sabotage even the most brilliant story. They'll be your watchful eyes, making sure your manuscript is as polished as a new sports car.

And cover designers are the artists who'll make your book cover a slam dunk. They'll create a visual masterpiece that captures the essence of your story and makes readers go "Wow!" They'll be your creative partners, helping you make a first impression that'll knock readers' socks off!

So, don't be afraid to bring in the pros and make your book a literary home run. They'll be your secret weapons, ensuring that your book stands tall among the competition. With their expertise, you'll have a winning team that'll make your book shine brighter than the lights of Times Square!

Remember, writing may be a solitary pursuit, but self-publishing doesn't have to be. Team up with the pros and let them be the MVPs of your literary journey. Together, you'll create a masterpiece that'll make readers cheer and your authorial dreams come true! Go team, go! U-S-A, U-S-A! *(Or any other country of your choosing!)*

Alright, let's talk about the "Publishing Hustle." It's decision time, and you've got options to consider. Traditional publishing, self-publishing, or hybrid publishing - which way are you gonna roll with?

Traditional publishing is like trying to score an invite to the most exclusive party in town. You gotta impress those gatekeepers, aka literary agents and publishers, with your manuscript and query letters. It's a slow dance of queries, rejections, and crossing your fingers for that elusive book deal. But hey, if you make it through the velvet ropes, you could be sipping champagne with the bigwigs of the publishing world.

Self-publishing is like being your own boss babe. You call the shots, from cover design to marketing strategies. It's like starting your own indie bookstore, but with your own book on the shelves. You gotta hustle hard, but you have the freedom to do things your way, and keep a bigger chunk of the royalties. Plus, you're in control of your own deadlines, which means more time for pizza and Netflix binge-watching.

Hybrid publishing is like the best of both worlds, like that perfect blend of coffee and almond milk. It's a mix of traditional and self-publishing, where you get the support of a publishing team while retaining some creative control. It's like having a literary agent as your wingman, helping you navigate the publishing world while still having the freedom to bring your own vision to life.

So, do your research, my bookish friends. Figure out which publishing path aligns with your bookish dreams and goals. Traditional, self, or hybrid - it's all about finding the right fit for you. Embrace the hustle, make your moves, and get ready to rock that publishing game like a literary boss! *#PublishingHustle #BookishDreams #BossBabeAuthor*

6. **Marketing Moves:** Get your book noticed in the crowded book world by making some marketing magic. Create a website, rock social media, host giveaways, and use every trick in the book to spread the word about your masterpiece.

Fellow bookish wizards, it's time to work some "Marketing Moves" to make your book shine in this crowded literary universe. Get ready to whip out your marketing wand and create some serious magic!

First up, the ultimate spell for book marketing success: create a killer website. It's like your book's online home base, where readers can get to know you and your masterpiece. Make it snazzy, make it sleek, and make it scream "pick me up and read me!"

Next, let's talk about social media sorcery. You gotta rock those platforms like a pro. Post about your book, share behind-the-scenes peeks, and engage with readers like they're your fellow Gryffindor pals. It's all about building that bookish tribe and making your book the talk of the town *(or the internet, in this case).*

And don't forget the power of giveaways, folks. Hosting bookish giveaways is like casting a spell to attract readers. Offer up some signed copies, bookmarks, or even a magical merch bundle, and watch the excitement unfold. It's like a Hogwarts feast for book lovers, and they'll be clamoring for a taste of your literary goodness.

Last but not least, use every trick in the book to spread the word about your masterpiece. Guest blog posts, book reviews, bookstagram shoutouts - you name it, do it! It's like waving your marketing wand and summoning readers to discover your book.

So, my bookish friends, get ready to work some marketing magic. Create a website that's as enchanting as a fairy tale, rock social media like a pro, host giveaways that'll make readers swoon, and use every trick in the book to spread the word about your literary gem. Get your marketing moves on, and let's make your book the talk of the bookish realm! *#MarketingMoves #BookishMagic #LiteraryGem*

6. **Formatting Finesse:** Make your book look as good as it reads! Pay attention to formatting details like margins, fonts, and spacing. A well-formatted book is a joy to read, and readers will love you for it.

   When it comes to self-publishing, don't forget to put on your formatting cowboy hat and wrangle those pesky details! A well-formatted book is like a rodeo clown that keeps readers entertained and coming back for more.

   Just like a rodeo cowboy needs to saddle up and get those ropes in line, you need to pay attention to the formatting details of your book. It's all about the margins, fonts, and spacing, y'all! A book that's easy on the eyes is a treat for readers, and they'll be hootin' and hollerin' for more.

   First, mind those margins like a vigilant sheriff keeping law and order in the Wild West. Too narrow or too wide margins can make your book look like a hot mess. So, measure 'em up and make sure they're just right, pardner!

Next, pick your fonts like you're at a hoedown, sifting through a sea of options. Go for legible fonts that are easy on the eyes and match the tone of your book. And steer clear of fancy fonts that'll make your readers squint like they're in the blazing sun without a hat!

And don't forget about spacing, y'all! Just like a cowboy needs enough room to swing his lasso, your text needs enough breathing space. Don't crowd your lines like a herd of cattle, but give 'em room to roam and make your book a joy to read!

So, round up those formatting details and give 'em the ol' rodeo treatment. A well-formatted book is like a lasso that keeps readers hooked from the first page to the last. They'll be tipin' their hats to you, and your book will be the talk of the town!

Remember, formatting finesse is the name of the game. So, saddle up, wrangle those details, and make your book look as good as it reads. Yeehaw, partner! Ride 'em high, and ride 'em proud!

7. **Beta Reader Bash:** Share your book with trusted beta readers who will give you honest feedback. Brace yourself for some tough love, but remember, it's all in the name of making your book even better!

Get ready to share your precious manuscript with some trusted beta readers and buckle up for some brutally honest feedback. It's like a literary reality show, and you're the star!

Think of your beta readers as your literary squad - they're the ones who will give it to you straight, no sugar-coating. Brace yourself for some tough love, but remember, it's all in the name of making your book even more epic. They'll point out plot holes, highlight awkward sentences, and give you the inside scoop on what's working and what's not. It's like getting a critique sandwich with a side of realness, and it's all in the name of leveling up your writing game.

But hey, don't take it personally. It's not a bookish roast, it's an opportunity to grow as a writer. Embrace the feedback with an open mind, and use it to polish your manuscript to perfection. It's like getting a makeover for your book, and it's gonna shine brighter than a diamond once you're done.

So, gather your trusted beta readers, send them your manuscript, and get ready for the feedback frenzy. It's a Beta Reader Bash like no other, and with their help, your book is gonna level up and slay the literary game. Keep calm, brace yourself, and let's make your book the best it can be! *#BetaReaderBash #LiterarySquad #FeedbackFrenzy*

8. **Formatting Frenzy:** Get your book formatted for print or e-book like a pro. Keep an eye on those margins, fonts, and spacing. Get ready to make your book look like a million bucks with some epic formatting skills. It's all about those margins, fonts, and spacing - the bookish trifecta for ultimate reader satisfaction!

Think of formatting like dressing up your book in its Sunday best. You gotta make sure those margins are on point, like they're ready for a red carpet premiere. No awkward white spaces or cramped text allowed. It's all about finding that perfect balance and making your book a visual feast for the eyes.

Fonts are the fashion statement of your book. Choose them wisely, my friends. You don't want your book to look like it's stuck in the '90s with Comic Sans or like it's screaming for attention with Papyrus. Pick fonts that are sleek, stylish, and easy on the eyes. It's like dressing your book in a designer outfit that's gonna turn heads on the literary runway.

Spacing is the dance partner of formatting. You gotta get that rhythm just right. Too much space and your book might look like it's taking a break, too little space and your readers might feel claustrophobic. It's like dancing to the beat of the literary gods, finding that sweet spot where your book flows smoothly and effortlessly.

So, my bookish comrades, get ready for a "Formatting Frenzy!" Keep those margins on point, choose fonts that are on-trend, and dance to the rhythm of perfect spacing. Let's make your book look like a million bucks, and readers will be eager to flip those pages in style! *#FormattingFrenzy #BookishStyle #MarginsMatters*

9. **Publishing Pizzazz:** Hit that publish button and watch your book go live! Celebrate with some confetti, dance like nobody's watching, and

get ready for the world to fall in love with your literary masterpiece.

It's a moment to celebrate, my friends - break out the confetti, put on your dancing shoes, and let loose like nobody's watching!

Hitting that publish button is like launching your book into the literary stratosphere. It's a thrill like no other, and it's time to own that moment. Imagine your book flying off into the virtual shelves, ready to captivate readers around the world. It's like releasing a literary rocket that's about to skyrocket to literary stardom.

So, when that publish button is clicked, it's time to party like a bookish rockstar. Dance like there's no tomorrow, and celebrate your literary masterpiece with all the pizzazz it deserves. Bust out the confetti cannons, pop the champagne *(or sparkling cider, if that's your jam),* and revel in the sweet satisfaction of seeing your book come to life.

But hey, the party doesn't stop there. Once your book is out in the wild, it's time to get ready for the world to fall in love with it. Embrace the feedback, engage with readers, and share your bookish journey with the world. It's like a literary love affair that's just getting started, and your publishing pizzazz is gonna keep the momentum going!

So, my fellow bookish comrades, get ready for some "Publishing Pizzazz!" Hit that publish button with gusto, celebrate like a rockstar, and get ready for your book to take the world by storm. It's time to shine like the literary superstar you are! *#PublishingPizzazz* *#BookishParty* *#LiteraryStarPower*

10. **Reviews Rollercoaster:** Brace yourself for the rollercoaster of emotions that is book reviews. Some will be rave, some will be meh, and some will make you question the meaning of life. Remember, not everyone will love your book, and that's okay. Keep writing, keep improving, and keep chasing your bookish dreams!

Brace yourself for a wild ride of emotions as you navigate the treacherous terrain of book reviews. Some will be rave, making you feel like you're floating on cloud nine with a virtual high-five from a delighted reader. Some will be "meh," leaving you scratching your head and wondering what went wrong. And then, there will be those reviews that make you question the very meaning of life itself. Yep, we've all been there.

But hey, here's the deal - not everyone will love your book, and that's okay. Taste is subjective, and even the most beloved books have their fair share of critics. So, when those not-so-glowing reviews come in, don't let them bring you down. Keep your chin up, your writing pen ready, and your bookish dreams alive and kicking.

Embrace the feedback, both positive and negative, as a chance to grow and improve as a writer. Learn from it, take what resonates with you, and let go of the rest. Don't let a few less-than-stellar reviews derail your writing journey. Remember, you're a literary warrior, and this is just a bump in the road of your bookish adventure.

Reviews are the lifeblood of authors. Embrace them, even the not-so-great ones. Learn from feedback, grow as a writer, and keep improving your craft. You've got this!

Reviews, they're like hot dogs, you gotta take the good with the bad. Yeah, it stings a little when you get a not-so-great review, but hey, you're an author, and you're made of tough stuff. Embrace the feedback, and use it as fuel to grow and improve your craft.

Sure, you might get a review that makes you roll your eyes so hard you see the Statue of Liberty from your window, but hey, that's part of the gig. Take a deep breath, pour yourself a cup of coffee *(or something stronger, we won't judge),* and read those reviews with an open mind. You might just learn a thing or two that'll make your next book even more kickass.

But don't stop there, buddy! Share the love for the good reviews. Show your appreciation for those readers who took the time to leave a glowing review. Give them a virtual high-five, or maybe even send them a pizza. Who doesn't love pizza, right?

And remember, you're not alone in this crazy writing journey. Connect with other authors, join writing groups, and share your experiences. Learn from each other, swap war stories, and commiserate over the woes of writer's block.

You've got a whole community of fellow writers who've got your back.

So, embrace the feedback, take it in stride, and keep on writing like the New York superstar you are. You've got this, pal! And remember, in the words of the great Frank Sinatra, "That's life, that's what all the people say. You're riding high in April, shot down in May. But I know I'm gonna change that tune when I'm back on top, back on top in June." Keep on writing, and keep on rocking!

So, my fellow bookish warriors, keep writing, keep improving, and keep chasing your bookish dreams with all your might. Ride the "Reviews Rollercoaster" with courage, resilience, and a sense of humor. After all, it's all part of the thrilling and unpredictable ride of being a writer. *#ReviewsRollercoaster   #BookishEmotions #LiteraryResilience*

Keep Writing, Keep Publishing! Congratulations, you're now on your way to being a certified author! But don't stop there. Keep writing, keep publishing, and keep sailing on the seas of literary success. Your next book might just be the next big thing!

Hey, you made it to the big leagues! You're a published author now, and that's no small feat. But hey, don't kick back and relax just yet. You've got the writing bug, and it's not going away anytime soon.

Keep those creative juices flowing, and keep that pen scribbling or those fingers typing. Don't let that fire inside you die down. Keep dreaming up those new story ideas, and let your imagination run wild like a taxi in rush hour traffic.

And hey, don't be afraid to hit that publish button again. You've got the hang of it now, right? Share your literary gems with the world and keep building your literary empire. Who knows, your next book might just be the one that skyrockets you to the top of the bestseller list, like the Empire State Building of literature.

But hey, it's not just about the fame and fortune. It's about the joy of creating, the thrill of storytelling, and the satisfaction of seeing your words come to life in the hands of eager readers. So, keep writing, keep publishing, and keep chasing your literary dreams like a New Yorker chasing a hot dog cart on a busy street.

And remember, even if you face some bumps in the road, like a pothole on a Brooklyn street, don't give up. Keep pushing forward, keep honing your craft, and keep believing in yourself. You've got the grit, the determination, and the talent to make it happen. So, keep writing, keep publishing, and keep conquering the literary world like a boss.

There you have it! Ten steps to publishing your own book like a millennial boss. It's gonna be a wild ride, but with passion, persistence, and a sprinkle of humor, you'll rock the literary world like a pro. Go slay those pages and make your mark on the bookish universe! *#AuthorGoals #BookishBoss #MillennialWriterVibes*

Broke Author's Guide to DIY: Saving Your Wallet and Your Sanity

If you're thinking about publishing your own book and don't want to break the bank, check out these 10 rad ways to save some serious dough:

1. **DIY cover art:** Instead of hiring a fancy-schmancy graphic designer, channel your inner Picasso and create your own wicked cover art. Canva and other free design tools got your back!

2. **Beta reader love:** Instead of hiring a pricey editor, gather your squad of grammar nerds to be your beta readers. They'll catch those typos and give you feedback for free!

3. **Digital format FTW:** Skip the printing costs and go all-in on digital format. E-books are hip and trendy, plus they save you moolah on printing and shipping.

4. **Crowdfunding magic:** Get your peeps excited about your book and crowdfund that bad boy! With platforms like Kickstarter and Patreon, you can rally your tribe and get some dough to fund your book dream.

5. **Social media hustle:** Embrace your inner social media guru and promote the heck out of your book on Instagram, TikTok, Twitter, and all the cool platforms. It's free marketing, baby!

6. **Print-on-demand awesomeness:** No need to print a massive batch of books and risk having them gather dust in your garage. Try print-on-demand services like Amazon's Kindle Direct Publishing or IngramSpark to save money on printing and storage.

7. **Collaboration power:** Team up with other indie authors and create an anthology. You'll share the costs of publishing and marketing, and have a blast working with other word wizards!

8. **Discount deals:** Keep an eye out for discounts and deals on printing, formatting, and other self-publishing services. There are always sweet deals to be found if you do your research.

9. **Library love:** Don't forget about your local library! They might be stoked to carry your book and help you spread the word, plus it's free exposure for your book!

10. **Book swaps, yo:** Connect with other indie authors and do some good ol' fashioned book swaps. You promote their book, they promote yours, and it's a win-win for everyone!

So there you have it, my fellow literary trailblazers and budget-savvy amigos! After exploring ten radical ways to achieve your publishing dreams without breaking the bank, you're now armed with the ultimate arsenal of money-saving techniques. So go forth into the world of self-publishing with your creative genius and financial prowess, and let those precious dollars stretch further than ever before! With your unwavering determination and frugal finesse, you're bound to rock that self-publishing game like a true champ, while keeping your wallet happy and your dreams soaring high. Get ready for an epic adventure of literary success and financial wizardry! 🎉 💰 📚 ✨

The Lazy Author's Guide to Online Selling: Let Robots Do the Work

Alright, so you wanna sell your digital products online but you're a total newbie and feeling less confident than a cat on roller skates. Been there, done that! It's not as easy-peasy as it sounds, especially if you're not a tech whiz.

But hey, fear not! There are some nifty online stores like **Smashwords** and **Payhip** that I use, where you can host your products without those pesky monthly fees. They just take a cut when you make a sale, which is perfect for us newbies on a budget. No tech knowledge needed, and you can start selling your goodies right away. It worked like a charm for me!

But if you wanna sell on your own website, which is totally legit and gives you major bragging rights, there are some sites out there that can help. They've got shopping carts and all these fancy automatic services to make your life easier. You can even design your own page, which is like putting a cherry on top of the cake. But here's the catch: they usually charge a monthly fee for their services, and I couldn't find any freebies *(bummer!)*. And honestly, with my untested products, I didn't wanna risk paying more in fees than what I could earn. No thank you, next!

So what I did instead was showcase my products on my own site and just add a link that takes buyers to my Smashwords and Payhip accounts when they're ready to purchase. Not the most ideal setup, I know, but a man's gotta do what a man's gotta do. Hosting it on my own site meant I couldn't accept payments and deliver products automatically, and I ain't got time to babysit my site 24/7, waiting for a sale. Ain't nobody got time for that! But hey, I'm not giving up on my quest for the holy grail of digital selling. Gotta keep hustlin' and find what works best for me! *#MillennialStruggles*

So, like, after searching high and low, I finally stumbled upon this site that's basically a godsend. Let me break it down for you, fam. You need a Paypal business account, but don't let the word "business" scare you off.

It's just a fancy term Paypal uses to separate personal and business accounts, and it's super easy to set up.

So, there are two types of accounts: personal and business. Personal accounts are for peeps who just want to use an online debit or credit card payment processor. On the other hand, the business account is for hustlers like us who are selling products or services online. But here's the catch - there's a fee for every transaction you make, but it's like minimal AF, and only when you actually make a sale. It's not like a "bye-bye to all your money" situation, promise.

Now, you might be thinking, "Well, why not just use online selling sites like Smashworld that also charge minimal fees?" And you're not wrong. But here's the tea - with Paypal, the payment goes straight into your Paypal account. No extra steps. Meanwhile, with other sites like Smashworld, you gotta transfer the money to your Paypal account anyway, and guess what? Paypal charges you AGAIN for the transaction, on top of the fees from the other site. Talk about getting charged twice!

However, Paypal has this slick feature where you can send buyers a download link right after they make a purchase. Like, you don't have to manually send the product or wait for the money to arrive in your Paypal account. It's all automated, which means you can focus on other things, like binge-watching your favorite series or perfecting your dance moves.

Using PayPal to Sell Digital Downloads

Here's what you need to do.

Step 1

Create your PayPal account and upgrade to a business account.

Step 2

Figure out where to put this file online like DropBox or Google Drive account.

Step 3

Upload your digital product to your Google Drive account. Right click on the file, or, when the document is open, click the Share button.

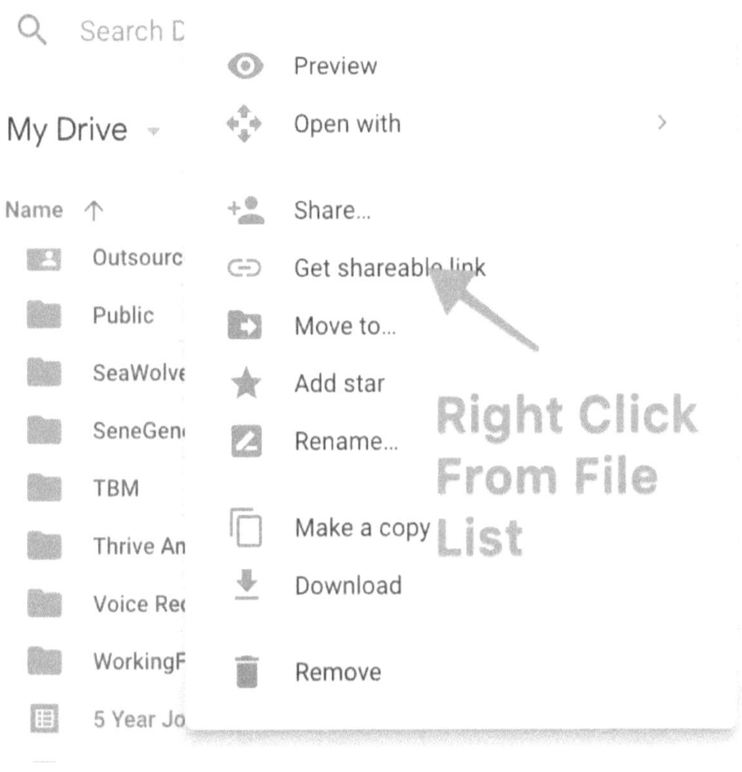

Q   Search D

Preview

My Drive ▾   Open with   >

Name ↑   Share...

Outsourc   Get shareable link

Public   Move to...

SeaWolve   Add star

SeneGen   Rename...   **Right Click**

TBM   **From File**

Thrive An   Make a copy   **List**

Voice Re   Download

WorkingF   Remove

5 Year Jo

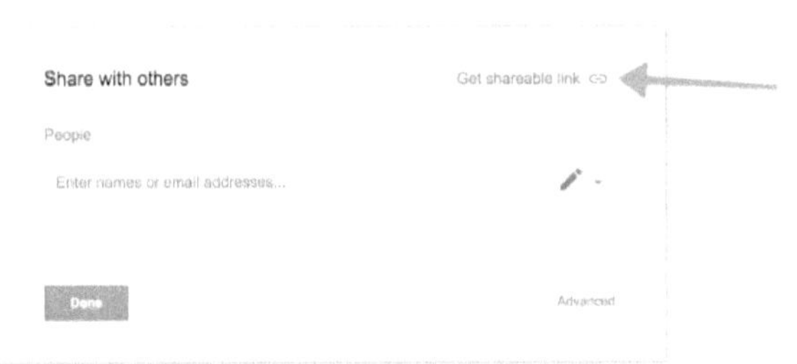

Step 4

Select the option where anyone with the link can view. Copy the link given and click Done. You will want to set aside this link for now.

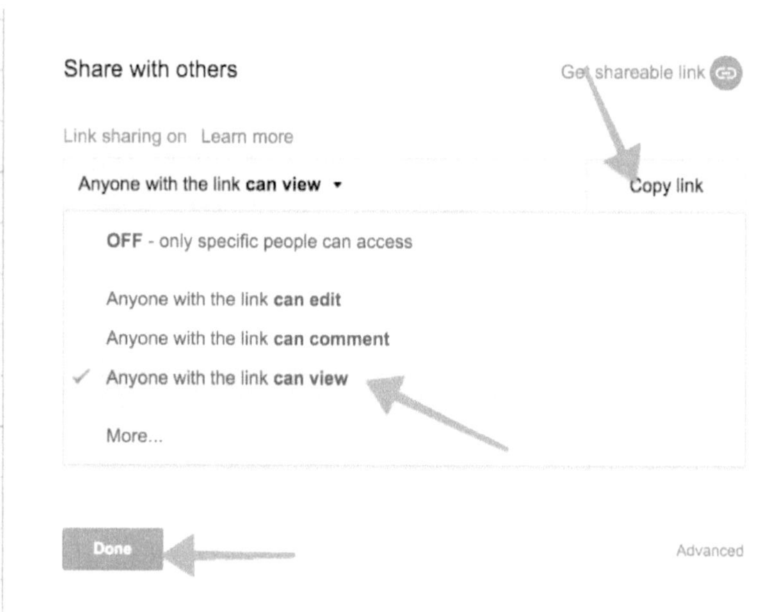

Step 5

Create a new Google Doc document. This will serve as your "pick up" page. This is what people will see after they have paid and redirected from PayPal.

Write something to thank your customer for their purchase. Tell them to click the link to download their purchase. Paste the link from the previous step into the document.

In the example below, we actually made a button inside Google Docs and make the button a link. Save your document. Repeat step 4 to get the shareable link for this document. Set it aside.

Thank You For Your Purchase!

Thank you so much for ordering the 5 Year Journal from me. My family and I appreciate your patronage. Click the button below to download your purchase.

Click To Download

Before You Go...

Check out this other product that would be a perfect match for your purchase.

FYI: *You can also create this page on your website or blog if you already have one.*

Step 6

Now it's time to create your PayPal button. Log into your PayPal account. Click the PayPal Buttons link from the drop down menu on the top.

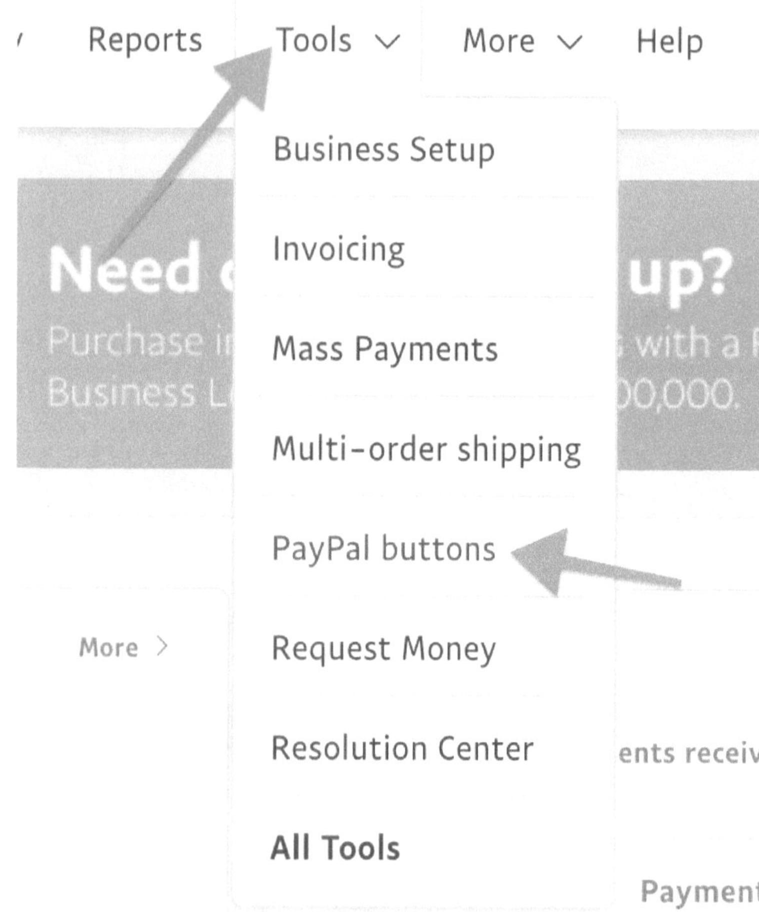
Reports
Tools
More
Help
Business Setup
Invoicing
Mass Payments
Multi-order shipping
PayPal buttons
Request Money
Resolution Center
All Tools
More
Payment
Completed
ents receive

Step 7

Choose the type of button you will create. In this example, we are creating a single buy button.

Step 8

Start configuring your button by giving it a name. This will show up for your customers in their receipt and account so you want to be clear. Give it a price. Most important at all, select the option to use the secure merchant ID.

Step 9

Click on the step 3 bar. You can skip step 2 in the button setup process since inventory is not necessary for digital products.

Step 2: Track inventory, profit & loss (optional)

Step 3: Customize advanced features (optional)

Create Button

Select no on the next two options since they are unnecessary.

You can set the shipping address to none unless you need it. Past the URL to your Google Doc into the field that says Take customers to URL when they finish checkout. Click Save.

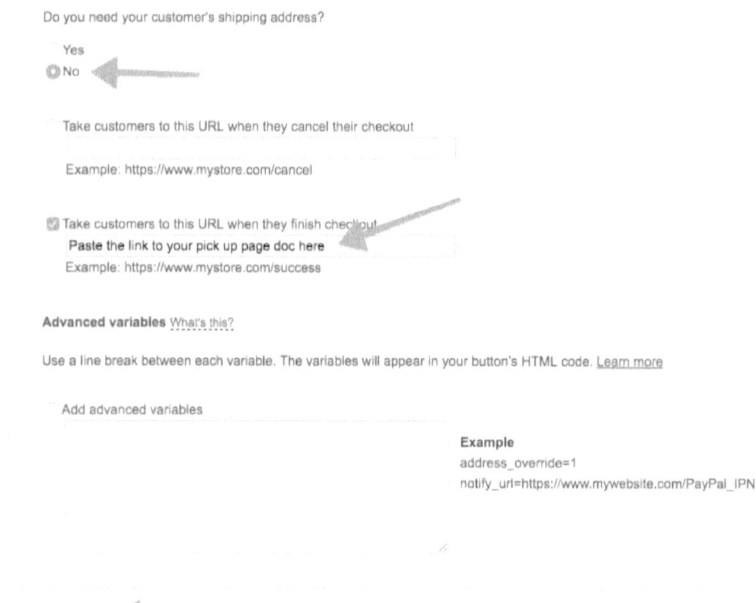

Step 10

On the next screen, you'll be shown your button code to put on your website. I prefer to grab just the link because it's more versatile. Now use this link on your own blog, web pages, signature link, social media and more.

Then, promote it like crazy!

And there's all there is to it. 10 simple steps

All's Well, Uhm But Not So Well

So yeah, I was stoked about this new automatic system to sell my stuff without wasting any extra cash. It was all smooth sailing until I hit a lil' bump with Paypal, especially 'cause I'm in the Philippines. And if you're in any country where Paypal is not that famous, we're on the same boat. Ugh, the struggle is real, my friends.

So, like, let me tell you about this online payment hustle I've been on, right? I was all stoked to use Paypal to sell my products online, but turns out, it's not really the go-to in the Philippines. GCash is like the cool kid on the block here. But here's the itsy-bitsy snag - although you can link GCash to Paypal, you can't straight up pay with GCash on Paypal. Talk about a buzzkill!

So, I hit up the interwebs again, and stumbled upon Paymongo, this supposedly all-in-one payment solution that accepts Visa/Mastercard, GCash, GrabPay, PayMaya, and more. I applied, but guess what? I still gotta submit some forms for them to approve my application. And I'm still waiting on GCash Getpaid to give me the green light too. But my main concern is, will these payment options let me send my products automatically like Paypal does? 'Cause in my back-and-forth with one of Paymongo's reps, they straight up admitted they don't have a system like Paypal's as of now.

Here's the tea - I've got the complete transcript of our convo right here:

On Mon, Dec 5, 2022 at 08:20 AM, "Augusto Meneses" <addmediacreatives@gmail.com> wrote:

Hi,

I have started my own small online shop and I wanted to provide customers with a way to pay directly to me (via my website) using gcash. Unfortunately I'm a simple layman and I can't comprehend all that mumbo-jumbo coding to create one for my site. Fortunately I came upon this very simple layman tech-help that enabled me to put a Paypal payment process right in my website (https://sites.google.com/view/makinganotherdaygreat/madgic-4-u/nsa-main?authuser=0). The good part is since I am offering digital products, there is also a way that my product gets sent to the buyer directly after payment and without me worrying about it.

Can your developers create something as simple as what Paypal can offer? Here's a link to it

https://techbasedmarketing.com/using-paypal-to-sell-digital-downloads/

The process is very simple and I have integrated it to my site already. Having something like this is a big boom to individuals that are just starting their own small business. If you have something similar to this already, please let me know so that I can use it on my site.

Thank you very much. If my suggestion comes as a nuisance to you, please accept my apology and dismiss my letter.

In it it says:

> **On Mon, Dec 5, 2022 at 08:20 AM, "Augusto Meneses" <addmediacreatives@gmail.com> wrote:**
>
> *Hi,*
>
> *I have started my own small online shop and I wanted to provide customers with a way to pay directly to me (via my website) using gcash. Unfortunately I'm a simple layman and I can't comprehend all that mumbo-jumbo coding to create one for my site. Fortunately I came upon this very simple layman tech-help that enabled me to put a Paypal payment process right in my website (https://sites.google.com/view/makinganotherdaygreat/madgic-4-u/nsa-main?authuser=0). The good part is since I am offering digital products, there*

is also a way that my product gets sent to the buyer directly after payment and without me worrying about it.

Can your developers create something as simple as what Paypal can offer? Here's a link *to it. The process is very simple and I have integrated it to my site already. Having something like this is a big boom to individuals that are just starting their own small business. If you have something similar to this already, please let me know so that I can use it on my site.*

Thank you very much. If my suggestion comes as a nuisance to you, please accept my apology and dismiss my letter.

Respectfully yours,

Augusto Meneses

I attached the screenshot of my conversation to prove that what I'm saying is legit and not a figment of my imagination. *Uhm, you know, just to make clear and to allay any suspicion from doubting Thomases.*

And here's the reply:

And here's the verbatim version:

> *Hi Augusto!*
>
> *Unfortunately, it is not yet possible but our engineers are close to launching a hosted checkout which is something similar to what you mentioned. Nevertheless, I'd be happy to flag this as a feature request for you!*
>
> *Please do let me know if you have any other feedback you'd like me to pass along!*
>
> *Your growth partner,*
>
> *Steven*

So, here I am, stuck in this predicament, trying to figure out how to use GCash as a payment option for my goods. I mean, Paymongo and Paypal ain't cutting it right now *(as of this posting)*.

GCash Comes To The Rescue *(uhm, sort of...)*

But then, a lightbulb moment! I found out that GCash lets you generate your very own QR code that you can slap on your site. So instead of just putting my GCash number out there, I've got this snazzy QR code that makes transactions official and puts my clients at ease. Shoutout to my tech-savvy son who's been using GCash since forever - we tested it out and it worked like a charm. Yehey!

Now I can accept GCash as a form of payment. But wait, wait, wait! How do I know who bought what and when? Sure, I can check my GCash transaction list but I was hoping for a better way. I am selling a lot of eBooks and I want to know which and what books are bought. There's no way I can do that by looking at my transaction details. Enter my daughter who asked, *"Haven't you used Google forms?"*

A Workaround For Online Selling

"Huh, what? Google forms — what's that?" I asked flustered.

My daughter gives me this odd look as if saying, *"are you a hermit or something, Dad?"* but still was patient enough to explain to me.

"A Google form," she began as if explaining to a 5-year old kid, *"allows you to create a form that could be used in your site."*

"Errr, how do I do that?" I asked.

With a sigh so deep, she huffed and puffed, she started to explain.

"First log into your Google drive," she said while looking at me suspiciously to see if I understand, *"You know that, do you?"*

"Of course, who doesn't use Google nowadays?"

She looked at me in an odd way, shook her head and then continued.

"To start with, you have to create a new Google form to use."

She goes on to explain that the form I will make would be filled up by my customer buying my eBook. Ang the best thing about it is that it could be linked to a Google sheet that will record each transaction as it happens. You can choose to make the Google sheet automatically or link the Google form with a Google sheet you made beforehand. You could link multiple forms in one Google sheet. Every form will have its own corresponding tab within the sheet.

Example of a Google form

1Day Order Form

Form description

Email *

Valid email

This form is collecting emails   Change settings

Name   Paragraph

Long answer text

                                                                                           Required

GCash Payment Reference Number *

Long answer text

The reference number can be found in the confirmation text sent by GCash

Description (optional)

Here's the steps on how to create an automatic Google sheet based on the Google form.

In your Google form, go to the tab *"Responses"* and select **"Response Destination."**

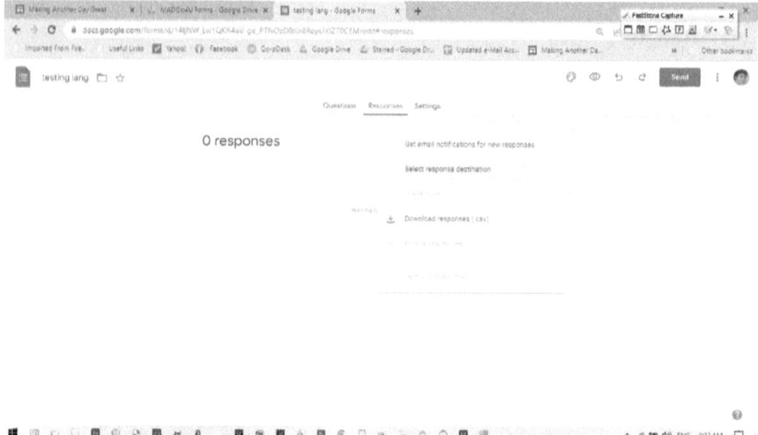

You will be presented with two choices, *"Create a New Spreadsheet"* and *"Select existing spreadsheet"*. The first option enables you to create a new spreadsheet based on the Google form which is currently open now. The second option gives you the choice to select an existing spreadsheet to link your Google form. In our sample, we will choose the option **"Create a New Spreadsheet."**

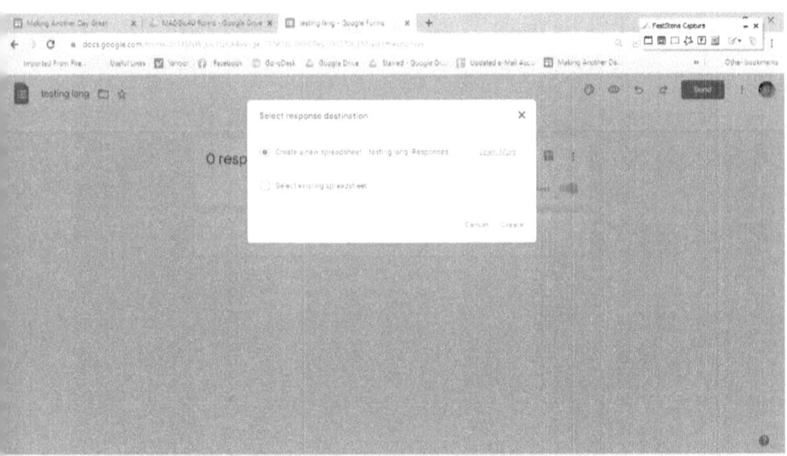

Which in turn creates this,

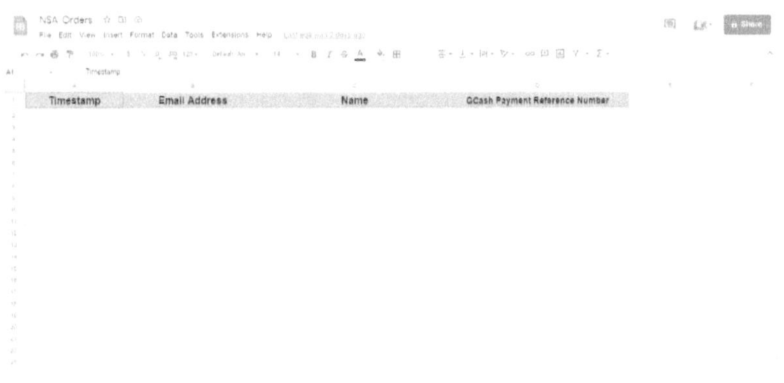

Hallelujah, God be praised! This is exactly what I wanted and needed! Now I will know exactly who bought my book and what. You could choose to put anything in your form but I recommend putting the following: **Name, Email Address**, and, in my case, the **GCash reference number**. You'll learn later on what the reasons are. Optionally, you could choose to add some requirements or conditions to your answer fields to make sure buyers fill it up correctly and lessen joy buyers.

So I've finished my form and got it ready to be imported to my site.

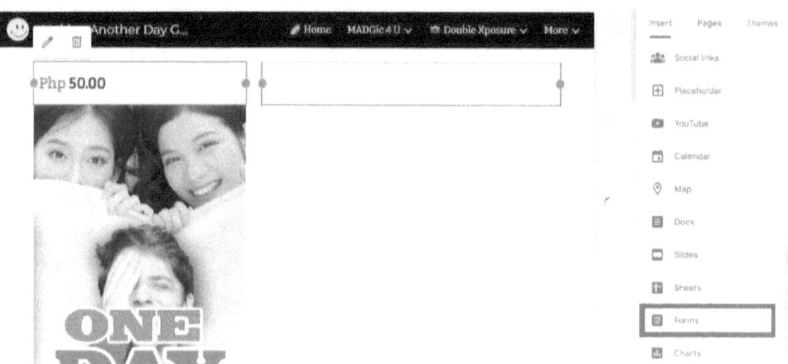

This is how it looks when placed with my custom designed page. This is how I arranged it, but you can opt to make your own design.

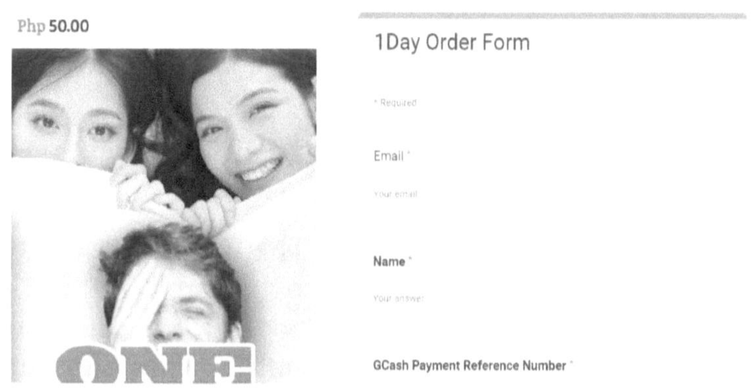

Ain't it a beauty!

Yo, yo, yo! I was on cloud nine, bro, when I finally got my setup all perfecto. But then, like, reality slapped me in the face when I remembered the struggle of sending those darn ePub files. Total bummer, man. Can't win 'em all, right?

Finally, My Online Store Is On Full Throttle

At least I've got GCash as my payment method and an auto-recording form in place. But dang, my inner Juan Tamad *(that lazy dude from Filipino folklore)* keeps nagging at me. There's gotta be a way to automate sending my books too, right? I mean, I solved the recording issue, so why not this one too? So, grumpy and all, I hit up the internet again to find a solution. And guess what? Lo and behold, I found one!

It's this online app that promises to create an auto response for every new entry in my sheet. I was stoked, so I gave it a shot. After a few trial and error attempts, I got it to work, kinda. Maybe I didn't follow the instructions to a T or something. I was at my wit's end, bro. So I mustered up the courage to ask my daughter for help. She asked me what app I was using, and when I told her, she was like, *"Dad, use __Autocrat__ instead."*

"Auto-what?" I asked. She gave me this resigned look like I'm a lost cause and explained that Autocrat does exactly what I want it to do.

I blinked, like, *"Hold up, am I hearing this right?"*

She nodded her head.

I so badly wanted to grab my daughter and have her teach me right then and there. But I played it cool like a harmless, obedient cat and meowed,

"Can you teach me...after your nap?" Which, knowing her, is probably gonna last till the end of the afternoon, if not longer.

So while I'm twiddling my thumbs, waiting for my princess to wake up, I went ahead and installed the Autocrat app on my Google browser. I don't need her to give me an earful for slacking off, you know what I'm saying?

But here's the catch, dude. Autocrat only works as an extension to Google browser and specifically Google Sheets. So if you're not on that train, better hop on now, bro.

Finally, after what felt like an eternity, my princess woke up on the right side of the bed, thank the heavens. She explained to me how Autocrat works and even showed me how to use it. But let me tell you, man, I'm struggling to keep up with all the steps. So she's like, "Don't worry, dad, I'll make a working model for you to follow." And she did, man! My site is now running like a charm, fully automated, and I can finally kick back and soak up the sun in the Riviera!

And now, without further ado, I'm passing on this knowledge to you, bro. But hey, just a heads-up, there might be other systems out there that are even better, man. I ain't saying my way is the best or foolproof. It's your call, bro. The risk is all yours, capisce?

First step. Install the Autocrat app and launch it. Oops, before starting, these are the items which are a prerequisite to make Autocrat work smoothly. First item, the Google sheet. Since I have started with the sample I made earlier, I will go with that. Make your own sample as you follow the instructions. That's one off the checklist. Next is the Google doc. You can make one like a thank you card, a receipt, or something but the important thing is that the download link to your file is there. This doc will be the template that will be converted to PDF and subsequently the file that will be sent to buyers. Finally, a folder in your Google Drive where all the PDF's will be nestled. The third one is optional but I recommend creating one and placing all the associated Autocrat files in it. This will make cross-checking easier going forward.

This is an example of the template using Google doc.

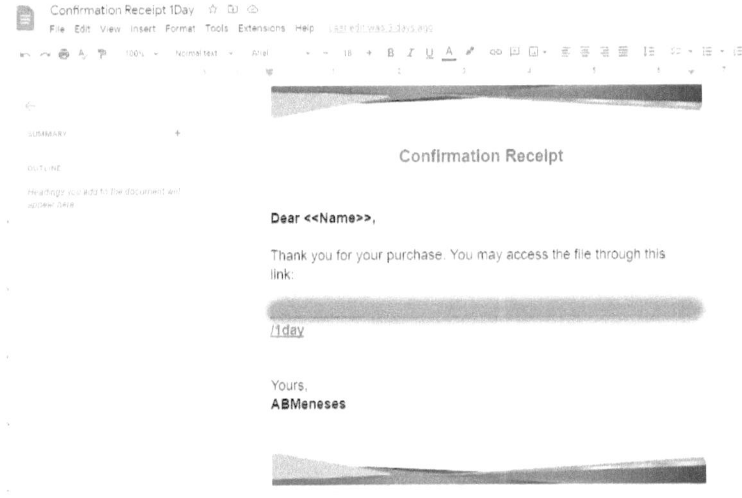

The << >> **tags** should contain exactly what appears in the header of your Google sheet. For example the column header **"Name"** wherein all the names of the buyers will be placed. This will ensure that new entries under the heading **"Name"** will be used.

Okay, is everything clear? Make sure that the Google sheet you made is open. Every Autocrat option will be based on it. **Hey, by this time you should have it installed already.** Now launch/open the Autocrat app. You can find it under the Extensions menu.

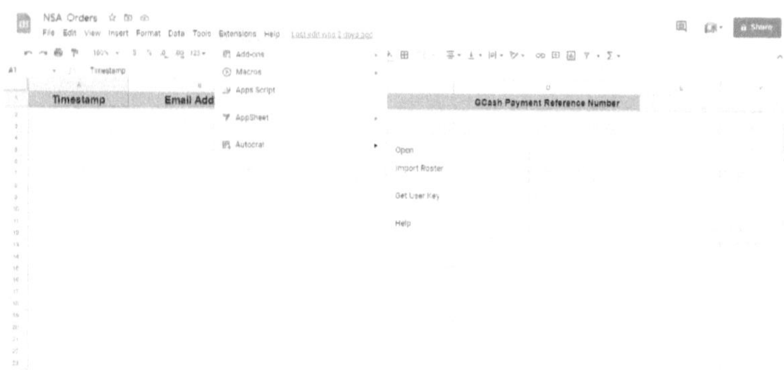

Next, as specified in the instructions, make a name for the merge job. The moment you save the project, the name will be listed in the lists of **"Existing Jobs,"** which will be presented every time the app is launched. After you finish or if you stop in the middle of the project, you can go back and edit it by clicking on the project name. You can also delete it if you want and start all over again. For the purpose of this exercise, I will name the project **1Day Confirmation Receipt.**

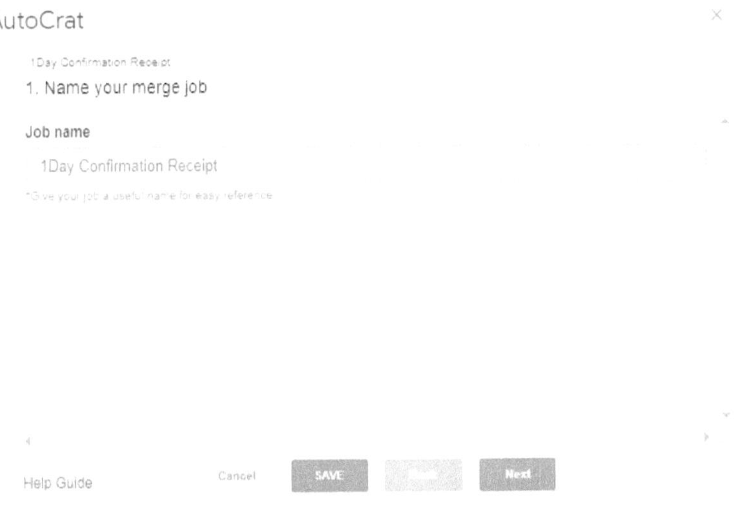

Next step. This is where I will need the Google form **"Confirmation Receipts 1Day"** I made earlier. As explained, this will serve as the template and subsequently the file that will be sent to the buyers.

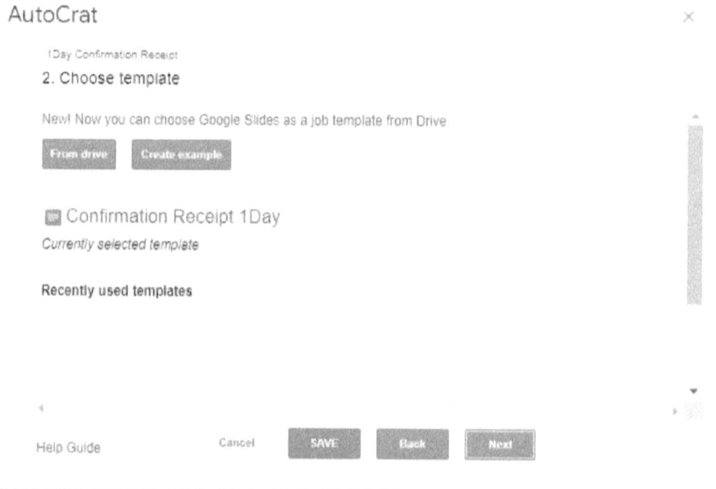

Step 3. Map the source data to template. This means that you will select the tab *(if you have multiple tabs in your sheet)* wherein Autocrat will be based. If there are no other tabs, then the single tab will be chosen automatically. In my example I have selected the 1Day tab. There's no need to change the other variables.

File setting. Here you will set the name of the file to be sent. In the File name section I opted to write **<<Name>> Order Confirmation to One Day ePub**. Make sure to select PDF as your file type. Select the output as Multiple output mode.

You can name your job to whatever filename you like but I recommend that you give it a name relative to the product you are selling. This will make it easier for you to remember it if it needs some editing in the future.

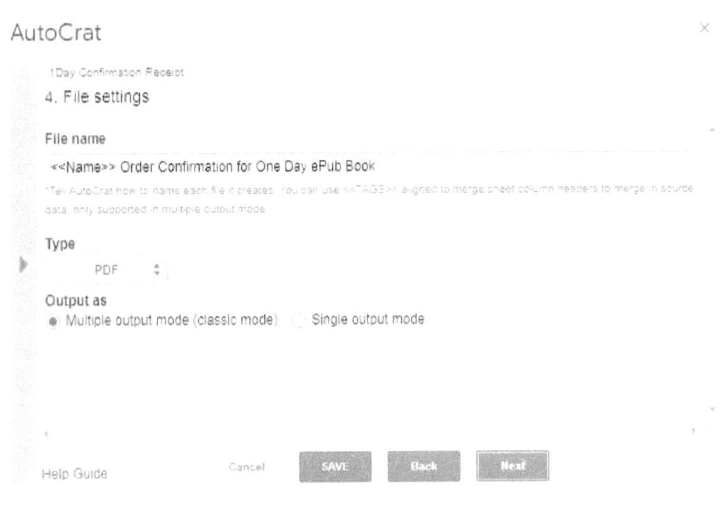

Choosing where to place your files. As I have stated earlier it is best that you assign a specific folder for all your Autocrat projects. This will make it easier for you to track down files if needed. Here I selected my Confirmation Order PDF folder I created earlier.

For our project we can **skip step 6**.

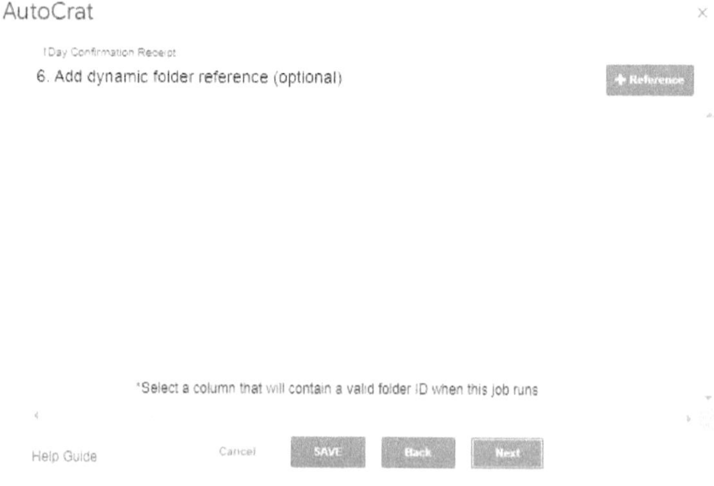

Again, we can skip **step** 7 also. Step 6 and 7 have no bearing to our project.

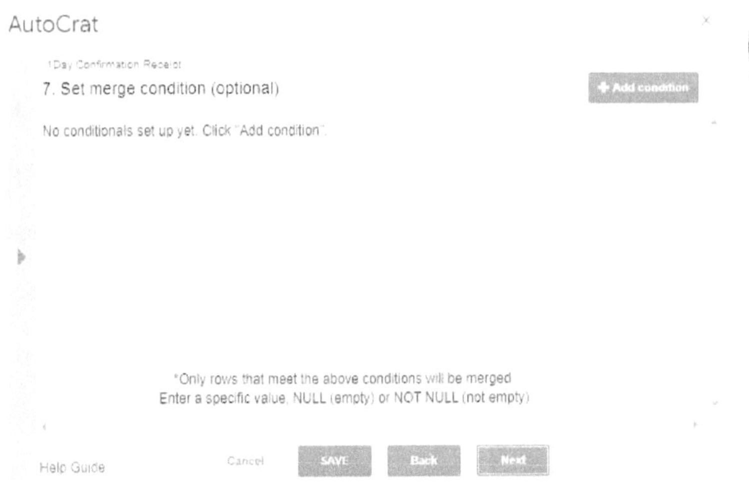

Step 8. This is it! The finishing touches. We are nearing the homestretch. Please follow exactly the instructions.

For the **Share doc?** Select **Yes.**

In the Share doc as, **make sure that PDF is selected**.

Allow collaborators? Select **No.**

Send from a generic address? Select **No.**

Scroll down to see the rest. You will need to fill out the subsequent form following it.

To: <<Email Address>> *(This will ensure that your mail goes to the correct recipient)*

NO NEED TO FILL OUT THE NEXT 3 LINES *(CC, BCC & REPLY TO).*

Okay, to continue...

Title: One Day ePub Order Confirmation *(or whatever your title is)*

Type your message to something similar like this:

Dear <<Name>>, *(the name of the recipient, your customer)*

Thank you for your purchase. Kindly open the attached PDF file for your confirmation receipt and access to the ePub book.

Best regards,

ABMeneses

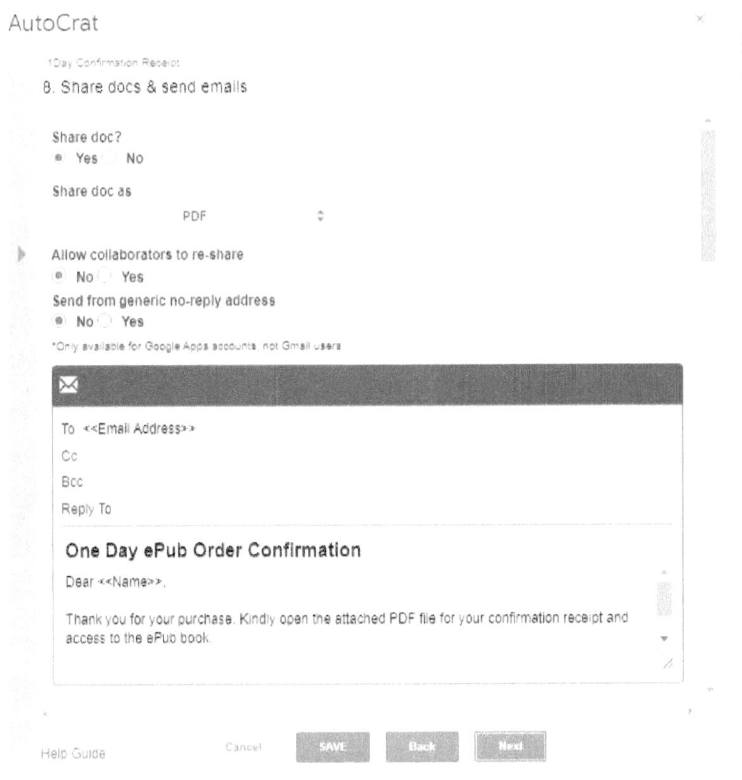

This is the 2nd most important part that you should not miss.

The trigger. This part will be the trigger to run the Autocrat instructions when a new entry enters the Google sheet.

Select **Yes** on **Run on form trigger**. (*This means that the form will activate when a new entry is entered in the Google sheet.*)

Select **No** on **Run on time trigger**

Click Save. Your Autocrat action job is now ready and set to go.

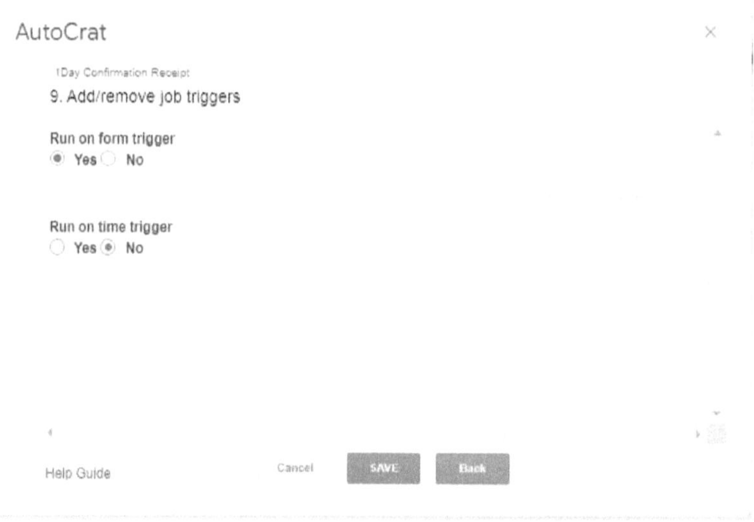

After you have saved your project, you will be directed back to the opening window when you first launch Autocrat. You will find your project listed in the **"Existing jobs"** list.

Make a test run. Fill out your Google form (Name, Email Address & GCash numbers) and submit it. With this action, you have activated the Autocrat app. Go to your Google sheet and you will find that the entries you have made in the Google form have been entered automatically in the Google sheet. The new entry will in turn trigger Autocrat to function accordingly.

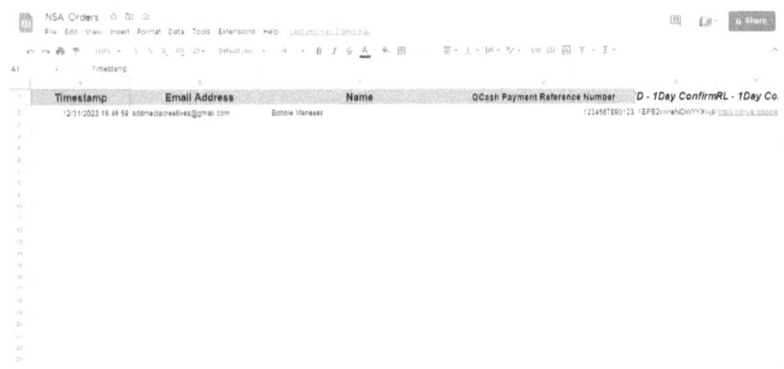

Check the email box you used in the submission. You will see that mail has been successfully sent to it.

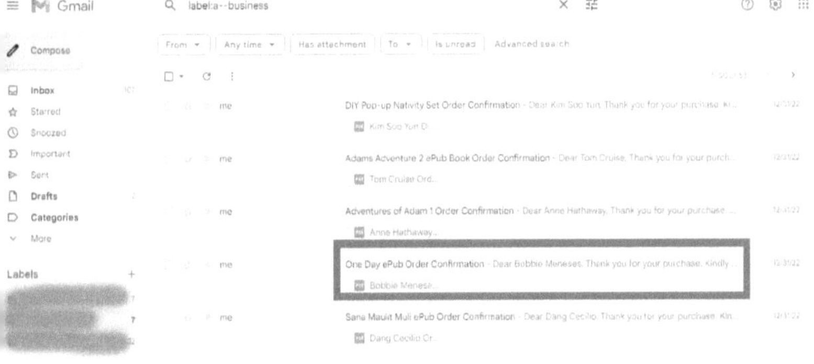

Open the mail. It will contain all the information you wrote in step 8. Open the attached PDF.

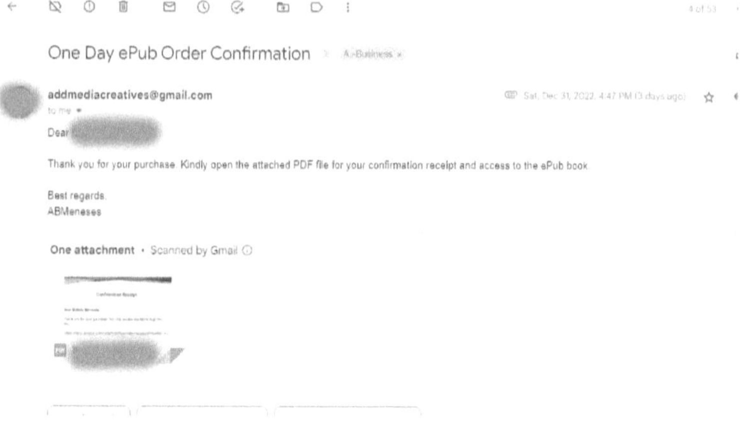

There it is, your confirmation receipt plus the link to the file download. All done automatically.

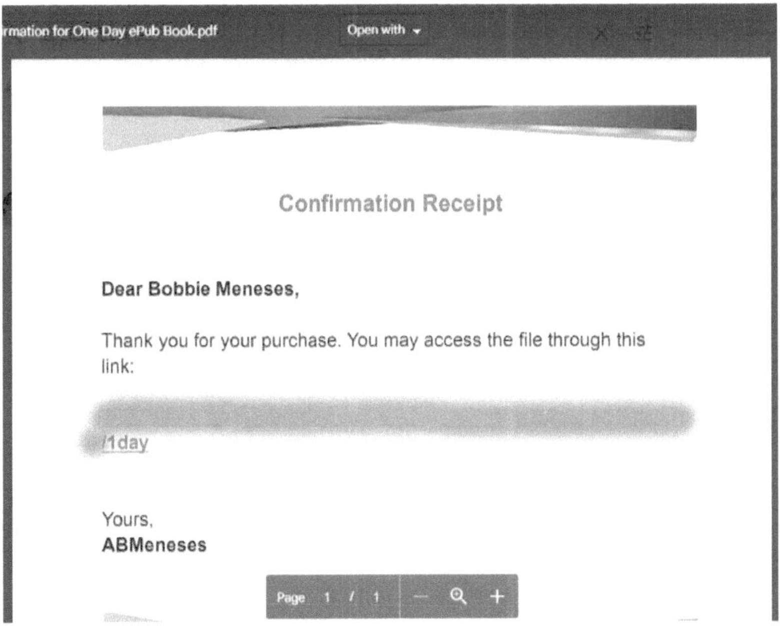

And of course, to complete the delivery, clicking on the link will get you here.

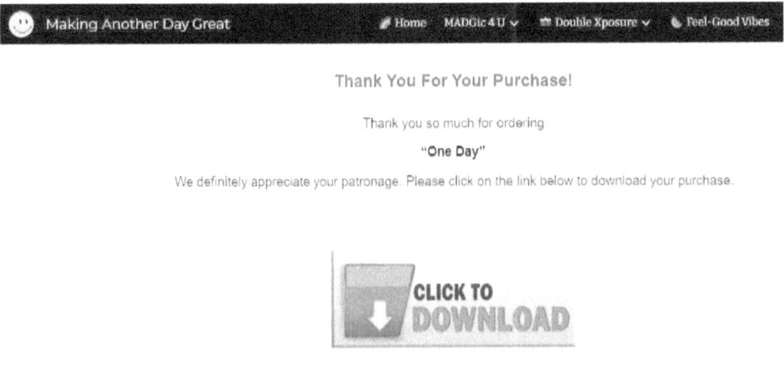

And finally here it is... delivery complete.

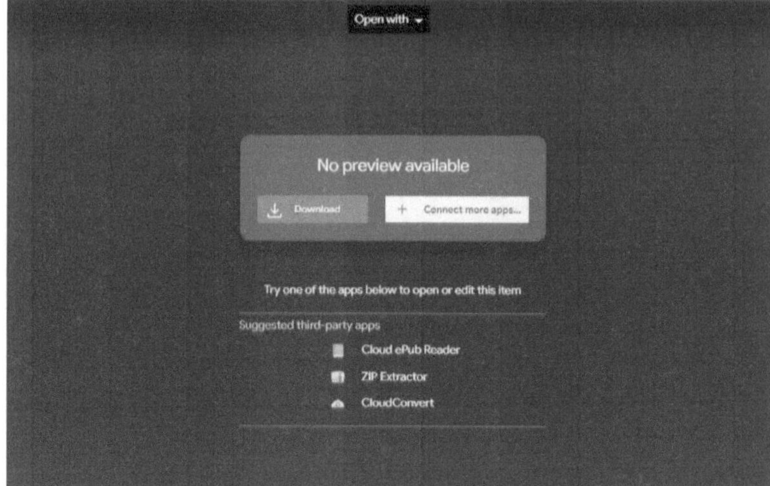

Viola, there you have it. A fully automated system.

Alright, listen up! Here's the deal: we've got a fully automated system for making money online, and yeah, it's not perfect, but it's fast and cheap. Sure, there might be some security risks, but let's be real, everything online comes with a little risk, am I right?

Now, I know you might be worried about whether people on your list have actually paid up, and that's a valid concern. But if you're just starting out, who needs high-tech security when you can focus on making that first sale? You can always hire an assistant to check on non-payers later, when you're raking in the big bucks. And let's face it, we're probably not selling out hundreds of copies right off the bat anyway, so let's keep it low-tech and hustle.

This method might not be great for selling a ton of products, but it's perfect for testing the waters with short-term products or doing some quick market research. If you're planning on selling a lot more, then yeah, it's time to invest in a fancy cart or system. And if recruiting affiliates is a must for you, well, skip this whole thing and start shopping for a system that's got that feature.

But hey, sometimes getting your product out there and making those sales is more important than getting everything perfect from the get-go. It's all about that proof of concept, you know? And taking too much time and spending all your profits on fees is a business killer. So why not start small, keep it simple, and see how the market responds? You don't need all the bells and whistles to make money online.

So come check out my online store and see how this system works for yourself. You might find something you like and want to buy, and hey, I'm here to help. Despite its flaws, this method definitely has its place in online marketing. Sometimes the fastest way to money isn't the prettiest, but it sure can be the most profitable. Best of luck with your sales! Peace out!

Crackin' the Autocrat Code: How the Magic Happens!

Hey there, curious minds! Ever wondered how this magical creature called "Autocrat" works its wonders? Well, buckle up, because we're about to take you on a wild and wacky ride through the mystical world of Autocrat! Get ready for a thrilling journey filled with automation, customization, and pure awesomeness. From merging data to generating personalized documents, Autocrat is like a supercharged wizard that can transform your workflow from tedious to terrific in a snap. So, hold on tight and let's unravel the mysteries of this enchanting tool together! ✨🌑🚀

Okay, here's the deal - Autocrat is like having a personal assistant that's always on fleek. It's this cool tech that hooks up with your Google Docs and Sheets, and it's like magic, man! You just set it up with some templates, and it cranks out all these customized docs and sheets for you. No more copying and pasting like a pleb, or spending hours tweaking the same report over and over again. Autocrat's got you covered, fam.

It's like having a boss that's a total autocrat, but in a good way. It's all about efficiency, yo. You just feed it some data, and it churns out all these fresh, polished docs and sheets that are ready to slay. And the best part? You can customize it to do whatever you want - from making invoices to sending out personalized emails. It's like a superpower, but without the cape and spandex.

So, instead of drowning in a sea of mindless busywork, you can let Autocrat handle the grind while you focus on being the genius that you are. It's like having your own personal minion, but without the weird yellow skin and goggles. Ain't nobody got time for repetitive tasks when you can let Autocrat do the heavy lifting, right? It's like having a BFF that's a productivity ninja, and who wouldn't want that in their squad?

In a nutshell, Autocrat is like having a boss that's a total rockstar and makes your work life a breeze. It's all about getting things done in a snap, so you can have more time for the things that really matter - like perfecting your TikTok dance moves or finding the best avocado toast in town. So, go ahead and let Autocrat be your productivity wingman, and watch your work game level up like a boss! *#AutocratGoals #WorkSmartNotHard*

GCash: Unleashing the Magic of Digital Wallets!

Hey there! So, let's talk about GCash - it's like having a digital piggy bank in your pocket that's cooler than your grandma's old-school coin jar. Basically, it's this super rad app that lets you do all sorts of money stuff with just a few taps on your phone. Let's dive in, shall we?

The advantage of GCash is that it's all about that sweet, sweet convenience. You can use it to pay for your fave online shopping hauls, split the bill with your squad after a late-night food run, or even pay your bills without having to deal with long lines or late fees. It's like having a money superhero in your pocket that saves the day, every day. *#MoneyHacks*

Oh, and get this - you can even send money to your fam and friends who have GCash too, no matter where they are. No more worrying about finding the nearest ATM or dealing with sketchy money transfer services. It's like having a teleportation device for money, but without the sci-fi stuff. *#MoneyMagic*

Plus, you can link your GCash to your bank account and cash in or cash out easily. It's like having your own personal ATM, but without the annoying transaction fees. You can even earn some sweet cashback rewards or get discounts when you use GCash for your purchases. It's like getting a bonus every time you spend money, and who wouldn't want that? *#CashbackCraze*

But, like with any app, there are a few things to watch out for. One of the disadvantages of GCash is that not all merchants accept it. So, you might not always be able to use it for all your shopping sprees or that trendy new café that just opened down the block. It's like when you can't use your favorite filter on a pic because your phone's storage is full. *#MerchantLimits*

Another thing to keep in mind is that GCash transactions are irreversible, just like that one bad tattoo you regret getting. So, double-check before you hit that send button, or you might end up sending money to the wrong person or getting scammed. It's like accidentally sending a risky text to your crush instead of your BFF. *#MoneyMistakes*

And while GCash is pretty awesome for digital transactions, it might not be the best option if you need to withdraw large amounts of cash or if you're in a place with spotty internet connection. It's like when your favorite streaming service keeps buffering during your binge-watching session. *#InternetWoes*

In a nutshell, GCash is like having a digital piggy bank that's super convenient and saves you from the hassle of cash and lines. It's all about that sweet, sweet convenience, money magic, and cashback rewards. But watch out for merchant limitations, irreversible transactions, and internet connection issues. Just like with anything else, it's all about finding the right balance and using it wisely. *#GCashGoals #MoneyMadeEasy*

Paypal: Unlocking the Magic of Money-Making Wizards!

Alright, so you've probably heard of PayPal, right? It's like Venmo's cooler, older sibling who's been in the game for longer. Basically, it's this app that lets you send and receive money online without all the hassle of dealing with cash or checks. No more IOUs or awkward "you owe me" texts. PayPal's got your back!

The advantage of PayPal is that it's super convenient. You can use it to pay for stuff online, split the bill with your squad when you're brunching it up, or even sell that old pair of sneakers you never wore. It's like having a digital wallet that you can take with you wherever you go. Plus, it's accepted by tons of merchants, so you can use it for all your online shopping sprees without having to enter your credit card info every time. *#Effortless*

But, like everything in life, there's always a catch. One of the disadvantages of PayPal is that it's not always free. Yep, you heard that right. There are fees for certain types of transactions, like receiving payments for goods and services, or converting currency. It's like finding out there's a hidden fee for extra guac on your burrito bowl. *#NotCool*

Another thing to watch out for is that PayPal transactions are irreversible. Once you hit that "send" button, there's no turning back. So, if you accidentally send money to the wrong person, or if that eBay purchase turns out to be a scam, you might be out of luck. It's like getting a bad tattoo - it's permanent, bro. #DoubleCheckBeforeYouSend

Also, not all merchants accept PayPal, so you might not always be able to use it for your online shopping spree or that cute vintage find on Instagram. It's like when your favorite coffee shop doesn't take Apple Pay, and you're left digging for spare change in your pockets. #MerchantLimitations

In a nutshell, PayPal is like a digital money superhero that saves you from the hassle of cash and checks. It's convenient, widely accepted, and great for online transactions. But watch out for fees, irreversible transactions, and merchant limitations. Just like with anything else, it's all about finding the right balance and using it wisely. *#PayPalPerks #MoneyMadeEasy*

Paymongo Unwrapped: Unraveling the Magic of Payments Made Easy!

Paymongo is like a digital wallet for the cool kids who are all about that hustle life. It's like having a virtual piggy bank that's got your back when you need to pay or get paid. Here's the lowdown:

Advantage-wise, Paymongo is all about making that money move. You can use it to accept payments for your side hustle, your Etsy shop, or even your dog-walking gig. It's like having your own digital cash register that's open 24/7, and you don't even need a fancy store to make it happen. *#HustleMode*

Plus, Paymongo makes it super easy for you to get paid. You can accept credit card payments, online banking transfers, and even payments from different e-wallets. It's like having a buffet of payment options at your fingertips, and you get to pick and choose what works best for you. *#PaymentParty*

Oh, and here's the cherry on top - Paymongo's got this rad feature called "Payment Links." It's like having your own personal money-making hyperlink that you can share with your customers through chat, email, or even on social media. It's like sharing a hilarious meme with your squad, but instead of laughs, you get paid. *#LinkUp*

But, like with any app, there are a few things to keep in mind. One of the disadvantages of Paymongo is that it's not as well-known as some of the bigger players in the payment game. So, your customers might be a bit hesitant to use it if they're not familiar with it. It's like trying to convince your squad to try a new hangout spot instead of their usual go-to. *#NewKidOnTheBlock*

Another thing to consider is that Paymongo charges fees for certain transactions, like credit card payments. It's like when you're at your favorite coffee shop, and you find out they charge extra for whipped cream on your drink. *#FeesFrustration*

And while Paymongo is all about making those money moves, it's not available in all countries just yet. So, if you're a globetrotting entrepreneur, you might need to find an alternative payment solution for your international customers. It's like when you're craving your favorite cuisine, but the restaurant is closed for the day. *#GlobalGoals*

In a nutshell, Paymongo is like a digital wallet for the hustlers who want to get paid on their own terms. It's all about that payment party, payment links, and convenience for your side hustle. But watch out for its lesser-known status, transaction fees, and availability in different countries. It's all about finding the right fit for your money-making game. *#PaymongoPower #HustleHarder*

Beyond the Bookshop: Harnessing the Power of Online Stores for Indie Authors

Discover a variety of online stores that can help you sell your books online, including popular platforms like Smashwords and Payhip. These platforms provide authors with the tools to publish, market, and sell their books to a global audience. Additionally, there are other platforms and marketplaces, such as Amazon Kindle Direct Publishing (KDP), Barnes & Noble Press, and Etsy, that offer unique features and opportunities for authors to reach readers worldwide. Each platform has its own set of advantages and disadvantages, so it's essential to research and choose the one that best aligns with your publishing goals and target audience.

Here's some more information about different online stores for selling books:

Smashwords: Smashwords is a popular ebook publishing and distribution platform that allows authors to self-publish and sell their books in various digital formats, such as ePub, MOBI, and PDF. It offers a wide distribution network to major ebook retailers like Amazon, Apple Books, Barnes & Noble, and more, making it a convenient option for reaching a broad audience.

Payhip: Payhip is an online platform that enables authors to sell their digital products, including ebooks, directly to customers. It provides tools for creating customizable online stores, setting prices, and managing sales, making it a user-friendly option for authors who want to have control over their sales process and keep a larger share of their profits.

Amazon Kindle Direct Publishing (KDP): Amazon KDP is a popular self-publishing platform that allows authors to publish and sell their books exclusively on Amazon's Kindle store. It offers a large customer base and global reach, making it a powerful platform for reaching readers worldwide. Authors can choose to enroll their books in Kindle Unlimited, a subscription service, and earn royalties based on the number of pages read by subscribers.

Barnes & Noble Press: Barnes & Noble Press is a self-publishing platform that allows authors to sell their books in both ebook and print formats on Barnes & Noble's online store. It offers tools for formatting and designing books, as well as distribution options for print-on-demand (POD) books, making it a viable option for authors who want to sell their books in print.

Etsy: Etsy is an online marketplace known for handmade and vintage items, but it also allows authors to sell physical books, zines, and other printed materials. It provides a unique platform for authors who want to target a niche audience interested in handmade or unique books.

These are just a few examples of online stores and platforms for selling books. It's essential to research and compare the features, pricing, and distribution options of different platforms to determine which one aligns with your publishing goals and target audience.

Here are some pros and cons of each online store/platform mentioned:

Smashwords

Pros

Wide distribution network: Smashwords distributes ebooks to major retailers like Amazon, Apple

Books, Barnes & Noble, and more, reaching a broad audience.

Author control: Authors have control over pricing, royalties, and distribution options.

Formatting assistance: Smashwords provides tools and guidelines for formatting ebooks, making it easier for authors to create professional-looking ebooks.

Cons

Limited sales channels: Although Smashwords distributes to major retailers, it may not have the same level of visibility or sales volume as some other platforms like Amazon.

Royalty fees: Smashwords charges a percentage fee on each book sold, which can impact an author's earnings.

Payhip

Pros

Direct sales: Payhip allows authors to sell ebooks directly to customers, providing more control over the sales process and potentially higher profits.

Customizable online store: Payhip offers tools for creating customized online stores, allowing authors to showcase their brand and books in a unique way.

Flexible pricing options: Authors can set their own prices and offer discounts or promotions as needed.

Cons

Limited distribution: Payhip does not have the same level of distribution as some other platforms, so authors may need to drive their own traffic to their online store.

Payhip transaction fees: Payhip charges transaction fees on each sale, which can impact an author's earnings.

Amazon Kindle Direct Publishing (KDP)

Pros

Wide customer base: Amazon is one of the largest online retailers, providing access to a massive customer base and potential for high sales volume.

Kindle Unlimited: Enrolling in Kindle Unlimited allows authors to earn royalties based on pages read by subscribers.

Print-on-demand (POD) option: KDP offers POD services, allowing authors to sell print versions of their books on Amazon.

Cons

Exclusivity: Enrolling in Kindle Unlimited requires exclusivity, meaning authors cannot sell their ebook on other platforms.

Competition: The sheer volume of books on Amazon can make it challenging for new authors to gain visibility and sales.

Royalty rates: Royalty rates for ebooks on Amazon can vary based on factors like book price and territories, which may affect earnings.

Barnes & Noble Press

Pros

Print-on-demand (POD) option: Barnes & Noble Press offers POD services, allowing authors to sell print versions of their books on Barnes & Noble's online store.

Wide distribution: Barnes & Noble Press distributes ebooks to Barnes & Noble's online store, reaching a sizable audience.

Formatting tools: Barnes & Noble Press provides formatting tools and guidelines for creating professional-looking ebooks.

Cons

Limited sales channels: Barnes & Noble Press may not have the same level of visibility or sales volume as some other platforms like Amazon.

Royalty fees: Barnes & Noble Press charges a percentage fee on each book sold, which can impact an author's earnings.

Etsy

Pros

Niche audience: Etsy attracts a niche audience interested in handmade and unique items, which can be a good fit for authors who create custom or artisanal books.

Customization options: Etsy offers customization options for creating a unique online store and showcasing books in a creative way.

Community engagement: Etsy has a strong community of buyers and sellers, providing opportunities for engagement and networking.

Limited to physical books: Etsy is primarily geared towards selling physical books, so authors looking to sell ebooks may not find it as suitable.

Competition: Etsy has a large number of sellers, so standing out in a crowded marketplace may require additional effort in terms of marketing and promotion.

Transaction fees: Etsy charges transaction fees on each sale, which can impact an author's earnings.

It's important to carefully consider thepros and cons of each online store/platform based on your specific needs and goals as an author. Factors to consider may include your target audience, genre, pricing strategy, marketing efforts, and personal preferences. It's also a good idea to research and compare the fees, royalties, and distribution options offered by each platform to make an informed decision.

In addition to the online stores/platforms mentioned, there are numerous other options available for selling books online, such as BookBaby, Draft2Digital, IngramSpark, and more. Each platform has its own unique features, advantages, and disadvantages, so thorough research and consideration are essential in choosing the right one for your book sales strategy.

Remember, selling books online involves more than just choosing a platform. It also requires effective marketing, promotion, and engagement with your target audience. Building a strong author platform, utilizing social media, email marketing, and other promotional efforts can all contribute to your success as a self-published author.

Overall, understanding the pros and cons of different online stores/platforms, and choosing the one that aligns with your goals and marketing strategy, can greatly impact your success in selling your books online.

Write on the Money: Stories of Self-Publishing Success

Fellow word warriors, listen up! We're about to dive into the world of successful self-published authors who are slaying the game and making us all green with envy.

These authors are the definition of DIY success, and they've got the writing chops and marketing savvy to prove it. So, grab your laptops, put on your comfy pants, and let's see what these literary rockstars did right!

"Indie Queen Hoover": Colleen Hoover is the queen of self-publishing, and she's got the romance genre wrapped around her little finger. She built a massive fan base by writing relatable characters and heart-wrenching love stories that tug at our heartstrings. Plus, she's a social media maven, using platforms like Instagram and TikTok to connect with readers and build a loyal following.

"Mystery Maverick Flynn": Blake Crouch is a master of suspense and thrills, and he's got the self-publishing game on lock. His "Wayward Pines" series gained a massive following, and his mind-bending plots and page-turning writing style keep readers coming back for more. He's also a pro at using Amazon Kindle Direct Publishing (KDP) to reach a wider audience and score major book deals.

"Fantasy Phenom Sullivan": Michael J. Sullivan is a fantasy author who turned self-publishing into a fantasy come true. His "Riyria Revelations" series gained a cult following, and he used Kickstarter to fund his books and build a dedicated fan base. He's also a master at engaging with readers on social media and building a community around his stories.

"Rom-Com Extraordinaire Reid": Penny Reid is the queen of witty rom-coms, and she's got self-publishing down to a science. She built a devoted fan base by writing unique and quirky romantic comedies that stand out in a crowded market. She's also a pro at building a strong author brand, using eye-catching covers and clever marketing to attract readers.

"Contemporary Conqueror Hoover": Tarryn Fisher is a contemporary fiction powerhouse who knows how to make self-publishing work for her. She's built a loyal following by writing raw and emotional stories that tackle tough issues. She's also a pro at using social media and book clubs to connect with readers and build buzz around her books.

"Sci-Fi Sensation Howey": Hugh Howey is a self-publishing success story in the sci-fi world. His "Wool" series gained a massive following, and he used Amazon's KDP platform to reach readers all over the world. He's also a master at marketing and promotion, using strategies like book bundles and limited-time offers to boost sales.

"Thriller Queen Burke": J.A. Konrath *(aka Jack Kilborn and Joe Konrath)* is a thriller author who's crushing it in the self-publishing game. He's known for his fast-paced and suspenseful stories that keep readers on the edge of their seats. He's also a pro at using social media and book pricing strategies to build his brand and reach more readers.

"Paranormal Prodigy Hocking": Amanda Hocking is a self-publishing sensation in the paranormal romance genre. She gained a massive following by writing addictive and swoon-worthy stories about vampires, werewolves, and other supernatural creatures. She's also a pro at using social media and book bloggers to generate buzz around her books.

"Memoir Maven Karr": Mary Karr is a memoirist who's made a splash in the self-publishing world. Her brutally honest and deeply personal stories have captivated readers and earned her critical acclaim. She's also a pro at connecting with readers on social media and using her unique author voice to build a strong brand.

"Cozy Mystery Guru Carlisle": Kate Carlisle is a cozy mystery author who's rocking the self-publishing scene. Her charming and witty stories set in small towns with quirky characters have gained her a loyal fan base. She's also a pro at engaging with readers on social media and using newsletter marketing to keep her fans eagerly anticipating her next release.

So, what do these self-published authors have in common? They're not just great writers, but they're also marketing wizards who know how to connect with readers, build a brand, and generate buzz around their books. They're masters of social media, book pricing, and promotional strategies, and they're not afraid to think outside the box to get their stories into the hands of readers all over the world. So, take notes, fellow aspiring authors, because these self-publishing dynamos have set the bar high, and they're showing us all how it's done! Time to unleash our inner writing rockstars and follow in their footsteps!

Laugh Your Way to Literary Genius: A Playful Guide for Aspiring Authors

If you're dreaming of becoming the next literary legend, why not take some inspo from these popular authors? They've slayed the writing game and captured our hearts with their epic stories. So, get ready to channel your inner bookish guru and embrace your writing vibes!

"Queen Rowling": Need we say more? This queen of wizardry and words, J.K. Rowling, has cast a spell on readers of all ages with her magical Harry Potter series. So, grab your wand (or pen) and let your imagination soar like a Nimbus 2000!

"Guru Green": With his insightful and witty prose, John Green has won over the hearts of young readers everywhere. From "The Fault in Our Stars" to "Paper Towns," his stories are like emotional rollercoasters that leave us laughing and crying at the same time. Get ready to tug at those heartstrings!

"Thrill Mastermind Flynn": If you're a fan of twisty thrillers, then Gillian Flynn is your go-to guru. Her dark and suspenseful tales like "Gone Girl" and "Sharp Objects" are a masterclass in crafting plot twists that leave readers on the edge of their seats. Prepare to give your readers some major plot whiplash!

"Swoonworthy Bardugo": Leigh Bardugo has won over fantasy fans with her intricate world-building and diverse characters. From the "Grishaverse" series to "Six of Crows," her writing is like a spell that transports readers to a magical realm filled with adventure, romance, and epic battles. Get ready to wield your literary magic wand!

"Quirky Queen Rowell": Rainbow Rowell is the queen of quirky, heartfelt stories that capture the awkwardness and beauty of growing up. Her books like "Fangirl" and "Eleanor & Park" are filled with relatable characters and unique perspectives that make us laugh, cry, and fall in love. Time to embrace your inner nerd!

"Mystery Maestro Lippman": Laura Lippman is the queen of mystery and suspense, with her complex characters and gripping plots that keep readers guessing until the very end. From her "Tess Monaghan" series to "Lady in the Lake," her books are like a puzzle that you can't wait to solve. Get ready to leave your readers on the edge of their seats!

"Sci-Fi Visionary Liu": Cixin Liu has taken the sci-fi world by storm with his epic "Three-Body Problem" trilogy. His mind-bending ideas and intricate world-building have earned him legions of fans. So, buckle up and get ready to journey to the far reaches of the universe with your own futuristic tale!

"Historical Maven Mantel": Hilary Mantel has brought history to life with her award-winning "Wolf Hall" trilogy. Her richly detailed and immersive historical fiction has earned her critical acclaim and a dedicated fan following. So, do some research, dust off your history books, and transport readers to a bygone era with your own captivating tale!

"Contemporary Wordsmith Ng": Celeste Ng has won over readers with her lyrical prose and poignant stories about family, identity, and race. Her books like "Little Fires Everywhere" and "Everything I Never Told You" are a masterclass in crafting emotionally resonant narratives. Get ready to tug at those heartstrings and leave your readers deeply moved!

"Rom-Com Extraordinaire Reid": If you're a sucker for romantic comedies, then look no further than Christina Lauren (the pen name for writing duo Christina Hobbs and Lauren Billings). Their heartwarming and hilarious rom-coms like "The Unhoneymooners" and "Roomies" are the perfect blend of swoon-worthy romance and laugh-out-loud humor. Get ready to make readers swoon and giggle with your own rom-com escapades!

So there you have it, fam! These popular authors have paved the way with their unique writing styles and captivating stories. Take a page from their books *(pun intended)*, find your own voice, and let your creativity soar. Whether you're into magic, mystery, romance, or any other genre, there's no time like the present to start crafting your own literary masterpiece. So grab your writing tools, sip on some coffee *(or matcha, if that's your thing)*, and let your words work their magic. You've got this! *#WritingInspo #LiteraryLegends #AuthorGoals*

Ink and Winks: A Humorous Look at the Ups and Downs of Publishing Books

If writing blunders abound, publishing mishaps may not be far behind, especially in the world of self-publishing! Brace yourself for a comical rollercoaster ride as we take a sneak peek at the hilarious adventures of DIY book publishing. From formatting fiascos to cover design calamities, it's bound to be an entertaining journey! So get ready for a laugh-filled ride through the whimsical world of self-publishing! 📚 😂 ✨

1. So, I finally self-published my book after spending hours agonizing over the perfect font and cover design. The excitement was real until I realized I made a typo on the first page! Talk about being a self-proclaimed grammar guru fail. *#EditorNeeded #Facepalm*

2. Turns out, writing the book was the easy part. Marketing it was a whole other ball game. I posted a selfie on Instagram with my book, trying to look all author-y and intellectual. But my friends' comments were like, "Wait, you can read?" *#AuthorGoals #ReadingIsCool*

3. I thought I had it all figured out with self-publishing until I discovered that Amazon has more categories for books than there are flavors of ice cream. I mean, who knew "Alien Invasion Time-Traveling Romance" was a thing? *#GenreConfusion #BookCategoryOverload*

4. I was so pumped to see my book on the shelves of a local bookstore, until I realized they only had one copy tucked between cat calendars and "how-to" guides on knitting. I guess I'll have to do some stealthy rearranging. *#BookstoreNinja #ShelfRealEstate*

5. I tried to save money by designing my own book cover, but I ended up with something that looked like it was made in Microsoft Paint by a drunk monkey. Lesson learned: hire a professional,

unless you want your book to scream "amateur hour." *#DIYFail #GraphicDesignNoob*

6. The joy of receiving my first book review quickly turned into a rollercoaster of emotions. "Brilliant! 5 stars!" But then I realized it was from my mom who hadn't read a book since the '90s. Love you, Mom, but can we get some unbiased opinions here? *#MomApproved #HonestReviewsNeeded*

7. I thought hosting a book signing event would be glamorous, but it turned out to be a struggle to get people to show up. I ended up bribing my friends with free pizza and drinks, and suddenly the turnout was record-breaking! *#PizzaIsTheUltimateMotivator #BookSigningBribery*

8. I was stoked to see my book available as an e-book, but then I realized that the preview on Amazon only showed the dedication page. Congrats to anyone who wanted to read a heartfelt shoutout to my cat! *#DedicatedToFluffy #BookTeaserFail*

9. I was all hyped up for a book launch party, but the only people who showed up were my aunt and her pet parrot. They were the most enthusiastic guests, though. Polly kept squawking "Buy the book!" all night. *#AwkwardButSupportive #BookLaunchPartyFlop*

10. After months of hard work, my book finally hit the bestseller list…in a super niche category with only 3 other books. I guess being the top seller in "Paranormal Llama Romance" isn't as glamorous as it sounds, but hey, I'll take it! *#UnexpectedBestseller #LlamaLoveStoryGoneWild*

E-Books Unleashed: The Good, The Bad, and The LOL-worthy of Different Digital Book Types!

Alright, peeps, let's talk e-books! We've got a bunch of different file formats to choose from, and each one comes with its own quirks. Time to break it down!

PDF

PDF: This one's like the OG of e-book formats, yo! It's like a digital printout of a book, with fixed formatting and all the graphics intact. Plus, it's compatible with almost any device, so you can read it on your phone, tablet, or laptop. But watch out, squad, 'cause PDFs can be a bit clunky to navigate, and they're not always great for smaller screens.

Pros: Fixed formatting, compatible with any device.

Cons: Clunky navigation, not ideal for smaller screens.

PDF stands for Portable Document Format, and it's like the OG of digital documents, yo! It's a file format that keeps your documents looking just like the original, with all the fonts, graphics, and formatting intact. And the best part? You can open it on almost any device, from your phone to your laptop to your tablet!

So, what can you use PDF for? Tons of things, fam! Here are some common uses:

Reading e-books: Many e-books come in PDF format, making it easy to read 'em on your preferred device. You can flip through the pages just like a physical book, and zoom in on text or graphics to get a closer look.

Sharing documents: Need to send an important document to your squad? PDF's got your back! You can create a PDF of a document, like a report, a resume, or a presentation, and send it to anyone, regardless of what device or software they're using. No more worrying about formatting getting messed up!

Forms and contracts: Say goodbye to printing, signing, and scanning documents, fam! Many forms and contracts come in PDF format, and you can easily fill them out electronically, add your signature, and send them back. It's like a virtual paperless office!

Archiving and preserving documents: PDF is great for archiving and preserving important documents, like legal contracts, financial records, or historical manuscripts. It ensures that the document remains in its original form, with no changes or edits, so you can refer back to it anytime you want.

Presentations and reports: Want to create a snazzy presentation or a professional report? You can use PDF to create polished documents with embedded images, charts, and other multimedia elements. Plus, you can easily share them with your team or clients for a sleek and professional look.

PDF is like the reliable, versatile, and widely-used file format that's perfect for reading, sharing, filling out forms, archiving, and creating professional documents. It's like the Swiss Army knife of digital documents, and it's got you covered for all your document needs! □□□

Ready to learn about some programs that can access PDF books? Let's dive in!

Adobe Acrobat Reader: This is the go-to program for opening and reading PDF books. It's free and widely used, offering a user-friendly interface with features like bookmarking, highlighting, and annotations. It's like having a trusty companion to navigate through the pages of your PDF books!

Microsoft Edge, Google Chrome, and other web browsers: Many web browsers have built-in PDF readers that allow you to view PDF books without needing to install any additional software. Simply open the PDF file in your web browser, and you're good to go. It's like having a built-in PDF viewer that's readily available!

Preview (Mac): If you're an Apple user, you're likely familiar with Preview, the default image viewer on macOS. However, it also has built-in PDF reading capabilities, making it a handy option for Mac users to access PDF books. It's like having a versatile tool for both images and PDFs!

Foxit Reader: This is another popular PDF reader that offers a range of features, including bookmarks, annotations, and form filling. It's known for its fast performance and lightweight design, making it a good option for those who want a streamlined PDF reading experience. It's like having a speedy and efficient PDF companion!

Nitro PDF Reader: This free PDF reader offers a range of features, such as bookmarks, text highlighting, and drawing tools, making it a versatile option for accessing PDF books. It also has a clean and intuitive interface, making it easy to use for both beginners and experienced users alike. It's like having a feature-rich PDF buddy!

With programs like Adobe Acrobat Reader, web browsers like Microsoft Edge and Google Chrome, Preview (Mac), Foxit Reader, and Nitro PDF Reader, you can access your beloved PDF books and embark on your digital reading adventures. Happy PDF reading!

ePub

ePub: This one's like the cool kid on the block! It's like a flexible format that adapts to different screen sizes and fonts. Plus, it's got built-in features like bookmarks, highlights, and even font customization. But hold up, peeps, 'cause not all e-readers support ePub, and sometimes the formatting can get wonky when you switch devices.

Pros: Flexible formatting, built-in features.

Cons: Not all e-readers support it, formatting may get wonky.

When it comes to e-books, we've got two main players: fixed layout ePub and reflowable ePub. Let me break it down for you, fam!

Fixed layout ePub is like a digital replica of a physical book, with set page sizes and fixed formatting. It's perfect for e-books that have complex layouts, like children's books or graphic novels, where the text and images need to stay in a specific place. The pros of fixed layout ePub are that it gives you more control over the design and allows for intricate graphics and formatting. It's like having a virtual replica of a physical book, complete with all the bells and whistles.

But yo, here's the catch: fixed layout ePub might not work well on all devices, especially smaller screens or e-readers. It can be a bit wonky on different screen sizes, and the text might not resize properly, which can be a bummer for readers who need to adjust the text size. Plus, the file size can be larger, which might make it slower to load or download, especially on slow internet connections. So, it's like a double-edged sword, fam!

On the other hand, reflowable ePub is like the cool, flexible cousin of fixed layout ePub. It adapts to different screen sizes and font settings, so it's all about that responsive design, yo! The text flows smoothly, and readers can adjust the text size and font to their liking, making it more accessible for peeps with different reading preferences or visual needs.

The pros of reflowable ePub are that it's versatile and works well on different devices, from e-readers to tablets to smartphones. It's also smaller in file size, so it's quicker to download and load. Plus, it's like the eco-friendly option, since it uses less data and storage space.

But here's the thing, fam: reflowable ePub might not be the best choice for e-books with complex layouts or intricate graphics, since the design might not be preserved perfectly. And some special formatting, like drop caps or text wrapping around images, might not work as smoothly. So, it's all about finding the right fit for your e-book!

To sum it up, fixed layout ePub is like the fancy option with full control over design, but it might not work well on all devices. Reflowable ePub is like the flexible and accessible option, but it might not be ideal for complex layouts. It's all about weighing the pros and cons, and choosing the format that suits your e-book's needs, fam!

Ready to dive into the world of e-books with reflowable and fixed layout EPUBs? Let's break it down and talk about some programs that can access these types of e-books!

Adobe Digital Editions: This popular software by Adobe is specifically designed for reading EPUBs, including both reflowable and fixed layout formats. It offers a user-friendly interface with customizable reading settings, such as font size, background color, and page layout options. It's like having your own personal e-book library at your fingertips!

Calibre: This free and open-source e-book management software is a go-to for many book lovers. It supports EPUBs in both reflowable and fixed layout formats and provides features for organizing, converting, and reading e-books. It's like a Swiss Army knife for managing your e-book collection!

iBooks *(Apple Books)*: If you're an Apple user, you're likely familiar with iBooks *(now Apple Books)*. It's the default e-book reader on iOS and macOS devices, and it supports both reflowable and fixed layout EPUBs. It offers a sleek and intuitive reading experience with features like bookmarks, highlights, and annotations. It's like having a personal e-book assistant on your Apple device!

Google Play Books: This is another popular e-book reader that supports both reflowable and fixed layout EPUBs. It's available on multiple platforms, including Android, iOS, and web browsers, making it accessible on a variety of devices. It offers features like night mode, font customization, and offline reading. It's like having your e-book library on the cloud, ready to be accessed from anywhere!

Kindle _(with conversion tools)_: While Kindle devices and apps are primarily designed for Amazon's proprietary e-book format (MOBI), they can also read EPUBs with the help of conversion tools like Calibre. However, keep in mind that the reading experience may not be as optimized as with EPUB-specific readers, as Kindle's focus is on their own format.

It's worth mentioning that some web browsers, like Google Chrome, also have built-in EPUB readers that can handle reflowable EPUBs. Simply drag and drop the EPUB file into the browser, and it will display the e-book for you to read.

So there you have it, folks! With programs like Adobe Digital Editions, Calibre, iBooks, Google Play Books, and Kindle (with conversion tools), you can access both reflowable and fixed layout EPUBs and embark on your digital reading adventures. Happy e-book reading!

HTML5

HTML5: This one's like the tech-savvy cousin of e-books, yo! It's like a web page disguised as a book, with interactive elements like videos, animations, and hyperlinks. Plus, it's super versatile and can be accessed on any device with a web browser. But be careful, fam, 'cause it might require an internet connection to fully enjoy, and not all e-readers support it.

Pros: Interactive elements, versatility.

Cons: Requires internet connection, not all e-readers support it.

Let's talk about HTML5, the latest and greatest version of Hypertext Markup Language that powers the web!

So, HTML5 is like the rockstar of web development, bringing in some serious improvements and cool features. The pros of HTML5 are:

Multimedia magic: HTML5 makes it super easy to add multimedia elements to web pages, like audio, video, and animations. No more relying on plugins or third-party software, fam!

Responsive design: HTML5 is all about that mobile-first approach, making it easier to create websites that look great and function smoothly on all devices, from smartphones to tablets to desktops. It's like web design on steroids!

Better semantics: HTML5 introduces new semantic elements, like <header>, <footer>, <nav>, and <article>, which make it easier to structure web pages and improve accessibility. It's like a language that speaks to both humans and search engines!

Offline access: HTML5 allows for offline caching, so you can still access web pages even when you're offline, like on a plane or in a dead zone. It's like web browsing on your own terms!

Performance boost: HTML5 comes with improved performance and efficiency, with features like Web Workers and WebSockets that make web apps faster and snappier. It's like a turbocharged web experience!

But hey, every coin has two sides, right? So here are some cons of HTML5:

Browser compatibility: Not all browsers fully support all the features of HTML5, so you might need to use workarounds or fallbacks for older browsers. It's like dealing with that one friend who's always lagging behind in the tech game!

Security concerns: With new features comes new potential security risks, and HTML5 is no exception. Developers need to be mindful of security best practices to prevent vulnerabilities and protect user data. It's like being the gatekeeper of the web!

Learning curve: HTML5 introduces new elements and syntax, which might require developers to learn new techniques and tools. It's like leveling up your coding skills!

Accessibility challenges: While HTML5 introduces better semantics, ensuring web pages are accessible to all users, it still requires careful consideration and implementation to meet accessibility standards. It's like building a web that's inclusive for everyone!

Constant updates: HTML5 is a dynamic standard that's constantly evolving, with new updates and versions being released. It's like trying to keep up with the latest trends in the fast-paced world of web development!

In a nutshell, HTML5 is like the superhero of web development, with its multimedia capabilities, responsive design, improved semantics, offline access, and performance boost. But like any superhero, it also has its challenges, like browser compatibility, security concerns, learning curve, accessibility challenges, and constant updates. It's all about leveraging its pros while addressing its cons to create amazing web experiences, fam! 💻 🌐 🚀

Flip-page

Flip-page format: This one's like a blast from the past, peeps! It's like a digital replica of a physical book, complete with page-flipping animations and realistic graphics. Plus, it's great for showcasing visual content like magazines or comics. But watch out, squad, 'cause it can be a bit cumbersome to read on smaller screens, and the page-flipping animations can get old real quick.

Pros: Realistic graphics, great for visual content.

Cons: Cumbersome on smaller screens, page-flipping animations can get old.

MS Word

MS Word: This one's like the DIY e-book format, fam! It's like using a word processor to create your own digital masterpiece. Plus, it's super customizable, so you can add your own fonts, images, and formatting.

But hold up, peeps, 'cause not all e-readers support MS Word, and the formatting might get lost in translation when you convert it to an e-book format.

Pros: Customizable, DIY vibes.

Cons: Not all e-readers support it, formatting may get lost in translation.

So there you have it! The lowdown on different e-book formats. From the classic PDF to the flexible ePub, tech-savvy HTML5, nostalgic flip-page, and DIY MS Word, each format has its pros and cons. So choose the one that fits your reading style and device, and get your e-book game on!

Enter the E-Reading Arena: Clash of the Titans Amongst Epic E-Book Readers!

Gear up for an electrifying showdown as we delve into the thrilling world of e-book readers! With a dazzling array of options to choose from, each one boasting its own unique strengths and weaknesses, the battle for e-reading supremacy is about to begin. From cutting-edge Kindles to versatile Nooks, and an array of other contenders vying for the crown, get ready for an epic clash of the e-reading titans! So buckle up, bookworms, and let's dive into the coolest showdown in town! 🏆 🔥 📖

The Classic E-Reader: This one's like the OG of e-books, ya know? It's like having a mini library in your pocket, with thousands of books at your fingertips. Plus, the e-ink screen makes it easy on the eyes, so you can read for hours without getting a headache. But watch out, peeps, 'cause these bad boys are pretty basic when it comes to features. No flashy apps or color screens here, just straight-up reading vibes.

Pros: Portable library, easy on the eyes.

Cons: Basic features, no fancy schmancy stuff.

The Tablet: This one's like the all-in-one package, yo! It's not just for reading, but also for binge-watching your fave shows, scrolling through social media, and playing games when you're taking a reading break. You've got all the bells and whistles, like color screens, adjustable font sizes, and even some interactive features.

But beware, squad, 'cause these babies can drain your battery faster than you can say "lit!"

Pros: Multi-purpose, fancy features.

Cons: Battery drain, distractions galore.

The Audiobook: Alright, so this one's like the lazy person's dream come true, no cap! You can listen to your fave books while doing other stuff, like hitting the gym, doing your makeup, or even just chilling on your couch. Plus, you get to enjoy some sick narrations by your fave celebs. But hold up, homies, 'cause you might miss out on the joy of flipping through actual pages and seeing those bookshelves filled with colorful spines.

Pros: Hands-free, celebrity narrations.

Cons: Miss out on flipping pages, no bookshelf swag.

The Interactive E-Book: This one's like a whole new level of reading, peeps! You can dive into interactive stories with choose-your-own-adventure vibes, where you get to make decisions that shape the plot. It's like playing a game and reading a book at the same time, which is pretty rad. But word of caution, squad, 'cause these books can get addictive AF, and you might end up spending hours just making choices and going down different storylines.

Pros: Interactive storytelling, game-like experience.

Cons: Addictive, time-consuming.

The Freebie E-Book: This one's like a budget-friendly option, squad! You can find tons of free e-books online, from classic literature to contemporary bestsellers. It's like a treasure hunt, yo! But watch out, 'cause not all free e-books are created equal. Some might have formatting issues, typos, or just not be your cup of tea. So choose wisely and don't judge a book by its "free" cover, fam!

Pros: Budget-friendly, treasure hunt vibes.

Cons: Quality may vary, formatting issues.

So there you have it, peeps! The lowdown on the different types of e-books. From classic e-readers to all-in-one tablets, lazy audiobooks to interactive storytelling, and budget-friendly freebies, there's something for everyone in the digital reading world. So pick your poison and get your read on! **Happy e-reading!** 📚😎✌️

Design Like a Pro: Game-Changing Tools for Crafting Stunning Book Layouts

Welcome to the world of book design wizardry! If you've ever dreamt of creating a visually stunning masterpiece that captivates readers from cover to cover, then you're in for a treat. In this guide, we'll explore some of the most powerful programs available for designing and laying out your book like a pro. From sleek and intuitive software to cutting-edge design tools, we'll unveil the secrets behind crafting visually appealing book layouts that are sure to leave your readers in awe. Whether you're a seasoned designer or a budding author looking to take control of your book's visual appeal, this is your ultimate guide to unleashing your creativity and designing a book that stands out from the crowd.

So, what are you waiting for? Go dive in and discover the game-changing tools that will elevate your book design to a whole new level!

Canva

The OG of book design apps. It's like a virtual arts and crafts store, but without the mess and the glue sticks. You can create beautiful book covers and interior layouts with just a few clicks. Plus, they have so many cool fonts and graphics, you'll feel like a design guru.

Alright, listen up, book lovers! If you're ready to slay the book design game without breaking a sweat, then Canva is your new BFF. Seriously, it's like having a magical design genie at your service.

First things first, Canva is as easy as swiping left on a dating app. You don't need a degree in graphic design or an IQ of 200 to figure it out. It's so user-friendly, even your grandma could rock it. Just sign up, pick your canvas size (hello, book layout!), and let the fun begin.

Oh, and the options? They're endless. Canva's got a treasure trove of pre-made templates for book covers, chapter headers, and more. Just drag and drop, customize with your own fonts and colors, and voila!

You'll have a book layout that's Pinterest-worthy and totally you.

But wait, there's more! Canva's got a massive library of free images, graphics, and clipart that'll make your book design pop like a party on New Year's Eve. You can search for anything from majestic mountains to adorable kittens, and add them to your layout with a single click. It's like having your own personal art gallery at your fingertips.

And did we mention the collaborations? Canva lets you invite your friends, your editor, your dog, whoever, to join in on the fun. You can work on your book layout together in real-time, leaving comments, making edits, and high-fiving each other for being design rockstars. It's like a virtual book design party, and everyone's invited!

But wait, there's even more! Canva's got a premium version with extra perks like access to premium images, unlimited storage, and the ability to resize your book layout for different platforms. It's like getting the VIP treatment for your book design dreams.

So, whether you're a budding author, a self-publisher, or just a book nerd with a knack for design, Canva's got your back. It's like having a design wizard in your pocket, ready to help you create a book layout that'll make your readers go "OMG, I need this book ASAP!" So why wait? Get your Canva on and let your book design shine like the star it is! ✹ ✺

Pros

User-friendly Interface: Canva offers a simple and intuitive interface that makes it easy for users of all skill levels to create professional-looking designs without any design experience.

Wide Range of Templates: Canva provides a vast library of pre-designed templates for various design purposes, including social media posts, presentations, posters, and more. This saves time and effort in creating designs from scratch.

Customizable Designs: Canva allows users to customize templates by easily changing text, images, colors, fonts, and other design elements to suit their specific needs and style preferences.

Access to Stock Images: Canva offers a large collection of free and paid stock images that users can use in their designs, eliminating the need to source images from external websites.

Collaboration Features: Canva allows users to collaborate on designs with team members or clients in real-time, making it a great tool for group projects or professional collaborations.

Cons

Limited Advanced Features: Canva may lack some of the advanced features and capabilities of professional design tools, making it less suitable for complex or intricate designs.

Paid Features: While Canva offers many free templates and design elements, some advanced features and premium stock images may require a paid subscription, which may not be suitable for users on a tight budget.

Branding Limitations: Canva's free version includes Canva's watermark, and removing it requires a paid subscription. This may not be ideal for users who want to create designs without any branding or watermarks.

Online-Based: Canva is a cloud-based design tool, which means users need an internet connection to access and use the software. This may not be convenient for users who need to work offline or in areas with limited internet connectivity.

Template Limitations: While Canva offers a wide range of templates, they may not always cater to specific niche or industry design requirements, which may require users to create custom designs from scratch.

In summary, Canva is a popular and user-friendly design tool with many benefits, such as its ease of use, wide range of templates, and collaboration features. However, it may have limitations in terms of advanced features, branding, and offline use. It's important to consider your specific design needs and budget when deciding if Canva is the right tool for you. Happy designing! 🎨✨🖌️

InDesign

Adobe's fancy-pants software for all you aspiring book designers. It's got all the bells and whistles, but beware, it can be a bit overwhelming if you're not used to playing around with design tools. But hey, you'll feel like a pro once you figure it out!

Alright, fellow bookworms, listen up! If you're ready to level up your book design game and slay the layout game like a boss, then Adobe InDesign is about to become your new BFF.

Think of InDesign like the Beyoncé of design software - it's fierce, powerful, and can make your book layout dreams come true. With InDesign, you can create jaw-dropping book designs that'll have your readers drooling over your mad design skills.

Now, let's talk about the features. InDesign is like a Swiss Army knife for designers. It's got all the tools you need to create sleek book layouts, from master pages that keep your design consistent, to powerful typography options that make your words look like poetry on the page. It's like having a design arsenal at your fingertips.

But wait, there's more! InDesign lets you play with images like a pro. You can import and manipulate photos, illustrations, and graphics with ease, and even create stunning image-driven layouts that'll have your readers swooning. It's like being a magician with images, pulling off mind-blowing tricks with just a few clicks.

And don't get me started on the creativity possibilities! InDesign lets you go wild with your artistic flair. You can experiment with different fonts, colors, and layout styles, and create a book design that's as unique as you are. It's like a playground for your creative genius, where the only limit is your imagination.

But wait, there's even more! InDesign is all about that teamwork. You can collaborate with your editor, your cover designer, and even your BFF who's got an eye for design, all in one place. You can leave comments, make edits, and have a virtual design party that's more fun than a TikTok dance challenge. It's like having your own creative squad, ready to help you make your book layout goals a reality.

So, if you're ready to up your book design game and create layouts that'll make your readers go "Wowza!", then InDesign is your secret weapon. It's like having a design superhero by your side, empowering you to create book layouts that are as epic as your story. So, grab your cape and let's get designing with InDesign, because your book layout is about to slay the design game like a boss! 💪🐊

Pros

Professional Design Features: InDesign is a powerful design software that offers a wide range of advanced features, such as precise layout control, typography tools, and image manipulation capabilities, making it ideal for professional-level design projects.

Layout Flexibility: InDesign allows users to create complex and multi-page layouts with ease, making it well-suited for designing print materials like books, magazines, brochures, and other publications.

Integration with Adobe Suite: InDesign seamlessly integrates with other Adobe Creative Cloud apps like Photoshop and Illustrator, allowing for easy collaboration and asset sharing among different design projects.

Print-Ready Output: InDesign provides robust print-ready export options, including high-resolution PDFs with advanced print settings, making it a preferred choice for professional print design projects.

Customization and Automation: InDesign offers extensive customization and automation options, such as master pages, styles, and scripts, which can greatly speed up the design process and ensure consistency across multiple pages or documents.

Cons

Steeper Learning Curve: InDesign has a steeper learning curve compared to some other design tools, requiring time and effort to master its advanced features and functionalities.

Expensive: InDesign is a part of Adobe's Creative Cloud subscription, which can be costly for users on a budget or those who only need occasional access to design software.

Overwhelming for Novice Users: InDesign's wide range of features and options may feel overwhelming for novice users or those with limited design experience, making it less accessible for beginners.

Resource-Intensive: InDesign requires a powerful computer system to run smoothly, including a robust processor, ample RAM, and ample storage space, which may not be feasible for users with lower-end hardware.

Not Web-Focused: InDesign is primarily designed for print and layout design, and may not be the best choice for web-focused design projects, such as website or app design.

In summary, InDesign is a powerful design tool with advanced features and capabilities, making it well-suited for professional print and layout design projects. However, it may have a steeper learning curve, be expensive, and have higher hardware requirements compared to other design tools. It's important to consider your specific design needs, budget, and level of expertise when deciding if InDesign is the right tool for you. Happy designing! 🎨 ✨ 🖌️

Scribus

Introducing the indie rock of book design software. It's free, open-source, and has a loyal following of designers who are all about that DIY vibe. Plus, you can brag about using a software that's not mainstream. Hipster points, anyone?

Alright, book nerds, listen up! If you're looking for a free, open-source design tool that's as cool as your fave indie band, then Scribus is about to become your new design crush.

First things first, Scribus is like a hidden gem in the design world. It's like finding a vintage vinyl record at a thrift store, except it's a design software that's totally free! Yep, you heard that right. No subscription fees, no hidden costs, just pure design awesomeness at your fingertips.

Now, let's talk about the design power of Scribus. It's like having a design wizard in your pocket, ready to work its magic on your book layout. You can create professional-looking book designs with its powerful tools for layout, typography, and image manipulation. It's like having a design powerhouse without breaking the bank.

But wait, there's more! Scribus is all about customization. You can tweak every little detail of your book layout to make it as unique as your rarest pair of sneakers. From custom fonts to personalized color schemes, you have total creative control to make your book design dreams come true. It's like having a virtual design playground where you're the boss.

And did we mention the community? Scribus has a rad community of fellow design enthusiasts who are always ready to help. You can find support in online forums, chat with other Scribus users, and learn from their design tips and tricks. It's like joining a design tribe that's got your back.

But wait, there's even more! Scribus is environmentally conscious, just like your eco-warrior bestie. It's all about sustainability, using open standards and supporting eco-friendly printing options. So you can design your book layout with a clear conscience, knowing you're making a positive impact on the planet.

So, if you're all about that indie vibe, and you're looking for a free, powerful, and community-driven design tool for your book layout, then Scribus is your go-to. It's like having a design bestie that's got your back, helping you create book layouts that are as unique as you are. So why wait? Let's get Scribus-ing and make your book design dreams a reality! 🎨📚

Pros

Open-Source and Free: Scribus is an open-source desktop publishing software that is available for free, making it an affordable option for budget-conscious users or those who prefer open-source software.

Layout Control: Scribus offers precise layout control with a wide range of professional design features, such as text and image manipulation, color management, and support for CMYK color space, making it suitable for print design projects.

Cross-Platform Compatibility: Scribus is compatible with multiple operating systems, including Windows, macOS, and Linux, allowing for flexibility in choosing the platform that works best for you.

PDF Export: Scribus provides robust PDF export options, including support for PDF/X-1a and PDF/X-3 standards, making it suitable for professional print production workflows.

Community Support: Scribus has a supportive user community, with active forums and online resources available for users to seek help, share tips and tricks, and stay updated with the latest developments.

Cons

Steeper Learning Curve: Scribus may have a steeper learning curve compared to some other desktop publishing software, as it requires familiarity with professional design concepts and terminology.

Limited Templates and Resources: Scribus may have fewer pre-designed templates and resources compared to other design tools, which may require users to create designs from scratch or source external templates.

Interface and User Experience: Some users may find the interface and user experience of Scribus less intuitive or user-friendly compared to other design software, which may require additional time and effort to get accustomed to.

Smaller User Base: While Scribus has an active community, it may have a smaller user base compared to more popular design tools, which may impact the availability of online tutorials, plugins, and support.

Limited Web Design Features: Scribus is primarily designed for print and layout design, and may not have as robust features for web-focused design projects, such as website or app design.

In summary, Scribus is a free and open-source desktop publishing software with powerful layout control and PDF export options, making it suitable for print design projects. However, it may have a steeper learning curve, limited templates and resources, and a smaller user base compared to other design tools. It's important to consider your specific design needs and level of expertise when deciding if Scribus is the right tool for you. Happy designing! 📰 ✨ ✏️

BookWright

This one's for all the Mac lovers out there. It's a user-friendly program that lets you design your book like a boss. It's got all the features you need, and the interface is so sleek, it'll make you feel like you're designing the next best-seller.

If you're ready to bring your book design game to the next level without breaking a sweat, then BookWright is about to become your new design BFF.

Picture this: you're a design prodigy with zero design skills. Well, fear not! BookWright is like your trusty sidekick that makes you look like a design rockstar without breaking a sweat. It's like having a personal design genie granting your book layout wishes!

Let's talk about the user-friendly vibes of BookWright. It's as easy as swiping left on a dating app (minus the awkward dates). You can drag and drop your way to a stunning book layout, without any coding or design jargon. It's like a design tool made for the Snapchat generation - quick, fun, and oh-so-easy to use.

But wait, there's more! BookWright is packed with creative goodies that'll make your book layout pop like a TikTok dance challenge. You can choose from a wide range of pre-designed templates, fonts, and graphics that are as trendy as the latest viral meme. It's like having a design stylist that'll keep your book layout on fleek!

And the best part? BookWright is all about customization. You can make your book layout as unique as your fave avocado toast order. From adjusting margins to tweaking typography, you have full control to make your book design as Instagrammable as your foodie pics. It's like having a design playground where you can unleash your creativity without any limits.

Oh, and did we mention the collaboration features? BookWright lets you team up with your fellow author buddies, editors, and even your mom who's got an eye for design. You can work together in real-time, leave comments, and have a virtual design party that's more fun than a Zoom quiz night. It's like a creative team-building exercise that'll make your book layout goals a reality.

So, if you're all about that user-friendly, creative, and collaborative design life, then BookWright is your go-to wingman. It's like having a design sidekick that's got your back, helping you create book layouts that'll make your readers go "wow!" So let's dive into the BookWright magic and make your book design dreams come true!

Pros

Easy-to-Use: BookWright offers a user-friendly interface with drag-and-drop functionality, making it easy for beginners to create professional-looking book layouts without extensive design experience.

Templates and Customization: BookWright provides a wide range of pre-designed templates for various book types, genres, and sizes, saving time and effort in creating book layouts from scratch. Users can also customize templates to suit their unique design preferences.

Integrated Publishing: BookWright allows users to publish directly to Blurb, a popular self-publishing platform, making it seamless to create, publish, and distribute books in print or digital formats.

Image Editing: BookWright includes basic image editing tools, such as cropping, resizing, and filters, which can be helpful for enhancing images within the book layout.

Collaboration and Sharing: BookWright allows for easy collaboration with co-authors or team members, and offers options for sharing drafts for review or feedback.

Cons

Limited Features: BookWright may lack some advanced design features found in other professional layout tools, such as InDesign or QuarkXPress, which may limit the customization options for more complex book layouts.

Platform Dependency: BookWright is a proprietary software tied to Blurb's self-publishing platform, which means that users may need to rely on Blurb for publishing and distribution, limiting flexibility in choosing other self-publishing options.

Limited Output Formats: While BookWright allows for creating print and digital book layouts, it may not have as much versatility in exporting to other file formats, such as e-book formats or print-ready PDFs for other printing services.

Learning Curve: While BookWright is designed to be user-friendly, users with no prior experience in book layout design may still require some time to learn and familiarize themselves with the software.

Cost: While BookWright is free to download and use, users may need to pay for printing and distribution services through Blurb, which can add to the overall cost of self-publishing a book.

In summary, BookWright is a user-friendly book layout tool with templates, customization options, and integrated publishing features, making it suitable for beginners or those looking for a streamlined self-publishing process. However, it may have limitations in advanced design features, output formats, and platform dependency. Consider your specific needs and goals when deciding if BookWright is the right choice for your book layout and self-publishing needs. Happy book designing! 📚✨✏️

Lucidpress

If you want a cloud-based solution that's as easy to use as Instagram, this one's for you. You can create stunning book layouts from anywhere, and collaborate with your team in real-time. Say goodbye to clunky desktop software and hello to sleek, modern design.

If you're ready to level up your book design game and slay those layouts, then Lucidpress is about to become your new design squad.

Okay, let's talk about the ease of use with Lucidpress. It's as simple as sliding into your DMs with a clever pickup line. You don't need to be a design guru to create stunning book layouts - Lucidpress has got your back with its sleek and intuitive interface. It's like having a design coach that'll guide you through every step without breaking a sweat.

But wait, there's more! Lucidpress is all about that creative flexibility. It's like a design buffet where you can feast on a wide range of templates, fonts, and graphics that are as trendy as your favorite TikTok dance challenge. You can mix and match, customize, and create a book layout that's as unique as your quirky personality. It's like having a design playground where you can let your creative juices flow without any boundaries.

And the best part? Lucidpress is all about that team spirit. You can collaborate with your fellow authors, editors, and even your long-lost pen pal from elementary school. You can work together in real-time, leave comments, and brainstorm like a creative powerhouse. It's like having a virtual design party where everyone's invited to bring their A-game.

But wait, there's more! Lucidpress also offers seamless integration with other popular design tools like Adobe Creative Cloud and Google Workspace. It's like having a design Swiss Army knife that can handle all your book layout needs in one place. You can easily import and export files, collaborate across different platforms, and keep your book design game strong.

So, if you're all about that easy-to-use, creatively flexible, and collaboratively awesome design life, then Lucidpress is your ride-or-die design squad. It's like having a design bestie that's got your back, helping you create book layouts that'll make your readers go "wow!" So let's dive into the Lucidpress magic and unleash your book design genius! 🚀 📖 ✨

Pros

User-Friendly Interface: Lucidpress offers a user-friendly interface with intuitive drag-and-drop functionality, making it easy for beginners to create professional-looking layouts for books or other print materials.

Collaboration and Sharing: Lucidpress allows for easy collaboration with team members, co-authors, or clients, making it ideal for collaborative book projects. It also offers options for sharing drafts for review or feedback, streamlining the feedback process.

Templates and Customization: Lucidpress provides a wide range of customizable templates for various print materials, including books, making it convenient for users to start with a pre-designed layout and customize it to their unique design preferences.

Cloud-Based: Lucidpress is a cloud-based tool, which means that users can access and work on their book layouts from anywhere, on any device with an internet connection, making it convenient for remote work or on-the-go design.

Integration with Other Tools: Lucidpress integrates with other popular design and collaboration tools, such as Google Drive, Adobe Creative Cloud, and Canva, enhancing its functionality and versatility.

Cons

Limited Advanced Design Features: Lucidpress may lack some advanced design features found in other professional design software, such as Adobe InDesign or QuarkXPress, which may limit customization options for complex book layouts.

Limited Output Formats: While Lucidpress allows for creating print-ready PDFs for books or other print materials, it may not have as much versatility in exporting to other file formats, such as e-book formats or other print-ready formats for different printing services.

Cost: While Lucidpress offers a free plan with limited features, access to more advanced features and functionality may require a subscription or upgrade to a paid plan, which can add to the overall cost of using the tool.

Learning Curve: Although Lucidpress is designed to be user-friendly, users with no prior experience in design software may still require some time to learn and familiarize themselves with the tool's features and functionality.

Branding: The free plan of Lucidpress includes branding of the Lucidpress logo on the published materials, which may not be desirable for professional or commercial book projects.

In summary, Lucidpress is a user-friendly cloud-based design tool with templates, customization options, and collaboration features, making it suitable for beginners and collaborative book projects. However, it may have limitations in advanced design features, output formats, and cost considerations. Consider your specific needs and budget when deciding if Lucidpress is the right choice for your book layout and design requirements. Happy designing!

Piktochart

Who said infographics were only for social media? With Piktochart, you can create eye-catching visuals for your book, from charts and graphs to timelines and diagrams. Spice up your pages with some data-driven bling!

Alright, let's talk about Piktochart - the good, the bad, and the funky!

Pros

Fresh and Funky Templates: Piktochart is all about those eye-catching visuals that'll make your book layout pop! With a wide range of trendy templates, you can create stunning infographics, charts, and graphics that'll have your readers hooked from cover to cover.

Drag-and-Drop Simplicity: No design degree needed here! Piktochart's intuitive drag-and-drop editor makes it easy for even the most design-challenged among us to create professional-looking book layouts. It's like playing with digital building blocks - you can easily add, resize, and customize elements with just a few clicks.

Customization Galore: Piktochart gives you the creative freedom to make your book layout truly yours. You can customize colors, fonts, backgrounds, and more to match your unique style and brand. It's like having a design genie that grants all your customization wishes!

Collaborative Vibes: Piktochart offers team collaboration features, so you can work with your co-authors, editors, or beta readers in real-time. You can leave comments, get feedback, and collaborate seamlessly to create the perfect book layout that'll wow your readers.

Cons

Limited Design Features: While Piktochart offers a wide range of templates and customization options, it may not have all the advanced design features that some professional designers crave. If you're looking for complex design tools or high-level customization, you may find Piktochart's options a bit limited.

Free Plan Limitations: Piktochart offers a free plan, but it comes with some limitations, such as a limited number of templates, watermark on exports, and limited storage. If you need access to more premium features, you may need to upgrade to a paid plan.

Learning Curve: While Piktochart is designed to be user-friendly, it may still take some time to get familiar with all the features and tools, especially if you're new to design. It may require a bit of trial and error to get the hang of it, but with some practice, you'll be designing like a pro!

Internet Connection Required: Piktochart is an online design tool, which means you'll need an internet connection to access and use it. If you're working offline or in an area with spotty internet, it may pose some challenges.

In a nutshell, Piktochart is a fresh and funky design tool that offers intuitive drag-and-drop simplicity, customization options, and collaborative features. While it may have some limitations in terms of advanced design features and free plan limitations, it can be a fun and creative tool for designing book layouts that'll make your readers go "wow!" So, grab your creative hat and let's get Piktochart-ing! 🎨 🗄 🚀

Visme

It's like a design playground for book nerds. You can create interactive and animated graphics that will make your book come to life. It's like adding a little sprinkle of fairy dust to your pages. Poof! Magic!

Oh, let's talk about Visme, the visual storyteller's dream come true! Here are some of the goodies that make Visme worth checking out:

Visual Versatility: Visme offers a wide range of visual content options, including presentations, infographics, reports, social media graphics, and more. You can create visually appealing book layouts with stunning graphics, charts, and images that'll make your readers swoon with awe.

Drag-and-Drop Simplicity: No design skills? No problem! Visme's drag-and-drop editor makes it super easy to create professional-looking book layouts without breaking a sweat. You can easily add, resize, and customize elements, and experiment with different layouts to find the perfect fit for your book.

Rich Media Integration: Visme lets you bring your book layout to life with rich media, including videos, audio, and interactive elements. You can add engaging multimedia elements to your book pages to create an immersive reading experience that'll keep your readers hooked.

Branding Brilliance: Visme allows you to maintain consistent branding throughout your book layout. You can easily upload your own brand assets, such as logos, fonts, and colors, and apply them to your book pages. This way, you can create a cohesive and professional-looking book layout that reflects your unique brand style.

Collaboration Features: Visme offers team collaboration features, so you can work seamlessly with your co-authors, editors, or beta readers in real-time. You can leave comments, get feedback, and collaborate on your book layout to create a masterpiece that's sure to captivate your readers.

Analytics and Privacy: Visme provides analytics and privacy features that allow you to track how your book layout is performing and protect your sensitive data. You can get insights on viewer engagement, shares, and more, and ensure that your book layout is secure and private.

Mobile Accessibility: Visme's mobile-responsive design makes your book layout accessible on various devices, including desktops, tablets, and smartphones. Your readers can enjoy your book on the go, giving them the flexibility to read wherever they are.

In a nutshell, Visme is a versatile, user-friendly, and visually appealing design tool that offers drag-and-drop simplicity, rich media integration, branding options, collaboration features, analytics, privacy, and mobile accessibility. It's a visual storyteller's paradise that can help you create stunning book layouts that'll captivate your readers and bring your book to life! 📖 🎨 🖌

Affinity Publisher

This one's for all the rebels who want an alternative to Adobe. Affinity Publisher is sleek, powerful, and oh-so-cool. It's got all the tools you need to make your book shine, without breaking the bank.

Is it worth the hype? You bet!

Pros

Professional-Grade Publishing: Affinity Publisher is a powerhouse design tool that offers professional-grade features for book layout and design. It's packed with advanced tools and features that can help you create stunning book layouts with precision and finesse.

Seamless Integration: Affinity Publisher seamlessly integrates with other Affinity software like Affinity Photo and Affinity Designer, creating a cohesive and efficient workflow for your design projects. You can easily switch between different Affinity apps, making it a breeze to create graphics, illustrations, and other design elements for your book layout.

Flexible Layout Options: Affinity Publisher offers a wide range of layout options, including multi-page spreads, text flow across pages, and flexible master pages. You can create complex book layouts with ease, and customize them to suit your unique style and content requirements.

Professional Typography: Affinity Publisher has a robust set of typography tools that allow you to create beautiful, professional-looking text layouts. You can easily apply advanced typography features such as drop caps, ligatures, and optical alignment to elevate the typographic quality of your book layout.

Image Editing Capabilities: Affinity Publisher comes with built-in image editing capabilities, allowing you to make adjustments and enhancements to your images directly within the application. You can crop, resize, apply filters, and perform other image editing tasks without needing a separate image editing software.

Non-Destructive Editing: Affinity Publisher's non-destructive editing feature allows you to make changes to your book layout without permanently altering the original content. This means you can experiment with different design elements and easily undo or modify changes, giving you more creative freedom and flexibility.

Cons

Learning Curve: Affinity Publisher has a steeper learning curve compared to some other design tools, especially if you're new to desktop publishing software. It may take some time to familiarize yourself with the interface, tools, and features, but once you get the hang of it, the possibilities are endless.

Limited Community and Resources: While Affinity Publisher has a growing community of users, it may not have as extensive a user base or resources as some other popular design tools. Finding tutorials, templates, and community support may require more effort compared to more widely-used software.

In conclusion, Affinity Publisher is a professional-grade design tool that offers powerful features for book layout and design. It has a learning curve but provides flexible layout options, professional typography, image editing capabilities, and non-destructive editing. If you're willing to invest the time to learn the ropes, it's definitely worth the hype and can be a valuable tool in your book design arsenal! 💪🎨✨

Microsoft Publisher

Yep, good ol' Microsoft is still kicking it in the book design game. It's like the classic denim jacket of design software - reliable, versatile, and always in style. Perfect for those who want something simple and familiar.

Microsoft Publisher, aka the OG of layout tools! It's like the cool uncle who's been around for a while and knows his stuff when it comes to creating snazzy book layouts.

Pros

User-Friendly Interface: Microsoft Publisher has a user-friendly interface that's easy to navigate, making it accessible for users of all skill levels. You don't need to be a design wizard to get started with Publisher.

Wide Range of Templates: Publisher comes with a vast library of pre-designed templates, from brochures to newsletters to booklets, making it a breeze to create professional-looking book layouts without starting from scratch.

Versatile Text and Image Tools: Publisher offers a wide range of text and image tools that allow you to customize your book layout. You can easily adjust fonts, colors, and styles, and add and manipulate images to create visually appealing designs.

Integration with Microsoft Office Suite: If you're already familiar with other Microsoft Office tools like Word or PowerPoint, you'll find Publisher's interface and workflow familiar and easy to use. You can easily import content from other Office applications, making it seamless to incorporate text and images into your book layout.

Print-Ready Output: Publisher allows you to create print-ready files, making it convenient for self-publishing authors who want to create physical copies of their books. You can set up bleeds, margins, and other print settings to ensure a professional-quality output.

Cons

Limited Advanced Design Features: While Publisher offers basic design tools, it may lack some of the advanced features and capabilities that are available in more robust design software. It may not be the best fit for complex book layouts or highly customized designs.

Compatibility with Non-Microsoft Users: Publisher files (.pub) are not widely compatible with other design software, which may pose challenges if you need to collaborate with designers or editors who don't have Publisher installed.

In summary, Microsoft Publisher is a user-friendly layout tool that's great for creating professional-looking book layouts with its wide range of templates, text and image tools, and integration with the Microsoft Office Suite. It may lack some advanced design features and compatibility with non-Microsoft users, but it's a reliable option for creating straightforward book layouts with ease. 📱📚✨

Pressbooks

If you want to self-publish your book, this one's a game-changer. It's a web-based platform that lets you design your book online and export it to various formats, like print, ebook, and PDF. It's like having your own personal book factory!

Pressbooks, the book layout genie, is a web-based platform that's specifically designed for self-publishers and authors who want to create beautiful book layouts without breaking a sweat.

Easy-to-Use: Pressbooks has a user-friendly interface that makes it easy for authors, even those with limited design experience, to create professional-looking book layouts with just a few clicks. It's designed with authors in mind, making it accessible and intuitive.

Customizable Templates: Pressbooks offers a wide range of customizable templates for various book types, including novels, textbooks, and poetry collections. You can choose from different fonts, colors, and styles, and easily customize the layout to suit your unique book design vision.

Collaborative Features: Pressbooks allows for easy collaboration with editors, designers, and other team members. You can grant access to different users and assign different roles, making it convenient for collaborative book projects.

Export to Multiple Formats: Pressbooks allows you to export your book layout to multiple formats, including PDF, EPUB, MOBI, and more. This makes it versatile for self-publishers who want to distribute their books in different formats and platforms.

Integrated Publishing: Pressbooks offers built-in publishing options, allowing you to publish your book directly to online platforms like Amazon Kindle, Apple iBooks, and more. This streamlines the publishing process and saves you time and effort.

Affordable Pricing: Pressbooks offers different pricing plans, including a free version with limited features and paid plans with more advanced features. This makes it accessible to a wide range of authors with different budgets.

In summary, Pressbooks is a user-friendly and customizable book layout tool that offers collaborative features, export to multiple formats, integrated publishing options, and affordable pricing. It's a convenient and efficient option for authors who want to create professional-looking book layouts without the hassle. 📚✨💻

Blurb

Don't let the name fool you, this one's actually pretty cool. Blurb is a self-publishing platform that lets you create beautiful books with their easy-to-use design tool. Plus, you can sell your books in their online bookstore and become the next Amazon best-seller. Ka-ching!

Blurbs, should you use it?

Absolutely, blurb it up! Blurbs are like little nuggets of bookish gold that can entice readers to pick up your book and dive into your story.

Pros

Book Marketing: Blurbs are a powerful marketing tool that can help you create buzz and generate interest in your book. A well-crafted blurb can hook potential readers and make them curious to know more about your story.

Reader Engagement: Blurbs give readers a taste of what your book is about and what they can expect from it. A compelling blurb can pique their interest and draw them into your story, increasing reader engagement.

Professional Appeal: Blurbs provide your book with a professional look and feel. They show that you've put thought into crafting a captivating description for your book, which can enhance its overall appeal to readers.

Competitive Edge: In a saturated book market, a catchy blurb can help your book stand out from the competition. A well-written blurb can differentiate your book and make it more appealing to potential readers.

Versatility: Blurbs can be used in various promotional materials, such as book covers, book listings, social media posts, and marketing campaigns. They are versatile and can be easily shared across different platforms to promote your book.

Cons

Limited Space: Blurbs usually have limited space, typically just a few lines or a short paragraph, to capture the essence of your book. Crafting a compelling blurb with limited space can be challenging, and it may not fully capture the complexity of your story.

Subjective Perception: Blurbs are subjective and depend on the taste of individual readers. What may be appealing to one reader may not resonate with another. It's important to strike a balance and create a blurb that appeals to your target audience.

In summary, using blurbs can be a valuable book marketing strategy that can help you create interest, engage readers, and give your book a professional edge. However, it's important to carefully craft your blurb to ensure it accurately represents your book and appeals to your target audience. So, blurb it up and watch your book shine! 📚 🎇 🔥

Lulu

Another self-publishing platform that's been around for a while, but still worth mentioning. Lulu offers a variety of book design templates and tools to make your book look like it came straight from a fancy publishing house. You'll be feeling like a big-shot author in no time.

Can a novice use Lulu?

Absolutely! Lulu is a user-friendly platform that is designed to cater to authors of all levels, including novices. With its easy-to-navigate interface and step-by-step publishing process, Lulu makes it accessible for beginners to create and publish their own books.

Pros

Simple Publishing Process: Lulu provides a straightforward publishing process that guides you through each step, from creating your book to formatting, cover design, and distribution. Even if you have little to no experience with book publishing, Lulu's intuitive platform makes it easy to get started.

Templates and Tools: Lulu offers a range of templates and tools that can help novices with book formatting, cover design, and other aspects of book creation. These resources can save time and effort in creating a professional-looking book without extensive design skills.

Print-on-Demand (POD) Printing: Lulu offers POD printing, which means your books are printed only when an order is placed, eliminating the need for upfront inventory or storage. This can be a cost-effective option for novice authors who want to publish their books without incurring high printing costs.

Publishing Options: Lulu provides various publishing options, including paperback, hardcover, and e-book formats, giving novices the flexibility to choose the format that best suits their needs and budget.

Distribution: Lulu offers distribution services, including listing your book on online marketplaces like Amazon, Barnes & Noble, and Lulu's own online bookstore, making it easier for novices to reach a wider audience.

Cons

Learning Curve: While Lulu is designed to be user-friendly, there may still be a learning curve for novices who are new to self-publishing or book formatting. It may take some time to understand the platform and its features, but Lulu does provide resources and support to help novices along the way.

Limited Design Options: While Lulu offers templates and tools, the design options may be limited compared to professional design software. Novices may need to work within the constraints of the available design options or seek external design help if they have specific design preferences.

In summary, Lulu is a user-friendly platform that can be used by novices to publish their books. With its simple publishing process, templates, tools, and distribution options, it can be a great option for novice authors looking to bring their stories to life. So, don't be afraid to give it a try and see your book come to fruition with Lulu! 📚 🚀 💫

MyCreativeShop

It's like a DIY design heaven. MyCreativeShop lets you create stunning book layouts with their drag-and-drop interface. Plus, they have tons of customizable templates to choose from, so you don't have to start from scratch. It's like having your own personal design assistant.

MyCreativeShop is primarily known for its online design tool that specializes in creating marketing materials like flyers, brochures, and social media posts. While it can be used for simple book layout and design, it may not be the best choice for more complex book projects.

Pros

Easy-to-Use: MyCreativeShop offers a user-friendly design tool that allows users to customize templates with their own text, images, and branding elements. It requires no design skills and can be a convenient option for simple book layout and design.

Templates and Customization: MyCreativeShop provides a wide range of templates for various types of books, including novels, children's books, and non-fiction. Users can customize these templates to fit their specific needs, making it easy to create visually appealing book layouts.

Online Access: MyCreativeShop is a web-based platform, which means you can access it from any computer with an internet connection. This can be convenient for authors who want to work on their book layout and design from different locations or devices.

Cons:

Limited Features: MyCreativeShop may not have all the advanced features and functionalities of professional design software, which could be limiting for complex book projects. It may not have the same level of control over typography, formatting, and other design elements that professional layout and design tools offer.

Print Quality: Since MyCreativeShop is an online design tool, the print quality of the final book may vary depending on the printing service used. It may not provide the same level of print quality and customization options as professional book layout and design software.

Book Formatting: Book formatting, including features like headers, footers, page numbering, and table of contents, can be more complex than what MyCreativeShop may offer. Authors may need to manually adjust these elements outside of the platform, which can be time-consuming and challenging for those without experience in book formatting.

In summary, while MyCreativeShop can be a convenient and easy-to-use option for simple book layout and design, it may not be the best choice for more complex book projects that require advanced features and customization options. It could be suitable for authors who are looking for basic book layout and design without the need for extensive formatting or customization.

Gravit Designer

For all you design geeks out there, this one's a treat. Gravit Designer is a vector-based design tool that lets you create intricate book layouts with precision. It's like a virtual canvas where you can let your creativity run wild and create masterpieces.

Gravit Designer is a vector-based design software that allows users to create graphics, illustrations, and other visual content. It offers a wide range of tools and features for designing various types of digital assets, including logos, posters, social media graphics, and more. Gravit Designer is available both as a web-based application and as a downloadable desktop app, offering flexibility in how and where users can create their designs.

Pros

Vector-Based Design: Gravit Designer uses vector graphics, which allows users to create scalable designs that can be resized without losing quality. This makes it suitable for designing graphics for different purposes and sizes, from small icons to large banners.

Robust Features: Gravit Designer offers a wide range of features, including tools for drawing, image editing, typography, and more. It also supports layers, blending modes, and other advanced design functionalities, giving users the flexibility and control to create intricate and professional-looking designs.

Cross-Platform Accessibility: Gravit Designer can be accessed as a web-based application, making it accessible from any computer with an internet connection. It also has downloadable desktop apps for Windows, Mac, and Linux, allowing users to work offline and sync their designs across multiple devices.

Free Plan Available: Gravit Designer offers a free plan with limited features, making it accessible to users who may be on a budget or just starting out with design. It also offers a Pro plan with additional features for more advanced design needs.

Cons

Learning Curve: Gravit Designer has a steeper learning curve compared to some other design tools, especially for users who are new to vector-based graphics or design software in general. It may require some time and effort to fully grasp its functionalities and capabilities.

Limited Collaboration Features: Gravit Designer's collaboration features are limited, which may not be suitable for larger design teams or projects that require extensive collaboration and real-time editing.

Offline Access Limited: While Gravit Designer offers downloadable desktop apps for offline access, some advanced features may require an internet connection.

This could be a limitation for users who frequently work in areas with limited or no internet access.

In summary, Gravit Designer is a powerful vector-based design software with a wide range of features for creating graphics and illustrations. It offers cross-platform accessibility and a free plan, but may have a steeper learning curve and limited collaboration features. It could be suitable for designers who are looking for robust design capabilities and flexibility in creating vector graphics for various digital assets.

Figma

If you're all about that collaborative life, Figma is the way to go. It's a cloud-based design tool that lets you work with your team in real-time, making book design a breeze, even if you're spread out across different time zones. Say goodbye to endless email chains and hello to seamless teamwork!

How do you use Figma?

Oh, Figma, the design tool of our dreams! Here's a quick rundown on how to use Figma like a pro:

Sign Up and Log In: First things first, create an account on Figma's website and log in to get started.

Create a New Project: Once you're in, create a new project to begin your design journey. You can choose from various canvas sizes, such as web, mobile, or custom dimensions.

Design on the Canvas: Figma's canvas is where the magic happens! You can drag and drop elements, such as shapes, images, and text, onto the canvas to create your design. Use the tools and features in the toolbar to customize your design to your heart's desire.

Utilize Layers and Components: Figma's layer and component system is a game-changer! Use layers to organize and structure your design elements, and create reusable components for efficiency and consistency across your design.

Collaborate with Others: Figma is all about collaboration! You can invite team members to your project, leave comments, and even work on the same design file simultaneously with real-time updates.

Share and Prototype: Once your design is ready, you can easily share it with others for feedback or present it to clients. You can also create interactive prototypes with clickable links and transitions to simulate user flows and test your design.

Handoff to Developers: Figma makes developer handoff a breeze! You can generate CSS, export assets, and even get design specifications to share with your development team.

Explore Plugins: Figma has an extensive library of plugins that can supercharge your workflow with additional tools, features, and integrations. Explore and install plugins that suit your needs to enhance your design process.

Stay Updated with Figma Community: Figma Community is a treasure trove of design resources! You can discover and access design files, UI kits, icons, and more created by the Figma community, and even share your own work to contribute to the design community.

Keep Learning and Exploring: Figma is a powerful design tool with a plethora of features and functionalities. Keep learning, experimenting, and exploring to make the most out of Figma's capabilities and create amazing designs!

Remember, practice makes perfect! So dive in, experiment, and have fun designing with Figma! Happy designing! 🎨 💡 🚀

Over

This one's for all you social media savvy book designers. Over is a mobile app that lets you create stunning graphics on the go. From book covers to promotional graphics, you can design like a pro right from your phone. Designing a book has never been this convenient, or this Instagram-worthy!

Oh, Over, the creative magic in your pocket! Over is a mobile app that empowers you to create stunning graphics, visuals, and designs right from your smartphone. It's like having a mini design studio in your pocket! Here's what you can do with Over:

Create Eye-Catching Graphics: Over offers a wide range of templates, fonts, images, and graphics that you can use to create beautiful social media posts, posters, invitations, logos, and more. You can customize and personalize your designs with your own text, colors, and images to make them truly unique.

Access a Massive Library of Assets: Over has an extensive library of millions of royalty-free images, graphics, and illustrations to choose from. You can search, browse, and select assets that fit your design style and theme, making it easy to find the perfect elements for your creations.

Add Text and Fonts: Over gives you access to a vast collection of fonts, allowing you to add text to your designs and customize it with various styles, sizes, and colors. You can create attention-grabbing headlines, quotes, and captions to make your designs stand out.

Edit and Enhance Photos: Over also includes basic photo editing tools, allowing you to adjust brightness, contrast, saturation, and other settings to enhance your images. You can also add filters, overlays, and effects to give your photos a professional touch.

Create Animated Designs: Over lets you add motion and life to your designs with its animation feature. You can animate text, graphics, and images to create engaging and dynamic visuals that capture attention and tell your story in a unique way.

Collaborate and Share: Over allows you to collaborate with team members and share your designs with ease. You can invite others to work on your designs or share your creations directly to social media, messaging apps, or email, making it easy to showcase your work and collaborate with others.

Save and Export: Once you're done creating your masterpiece, you can save it to your device or export it in various formats, such as JPEG, PNG, or GIF. You can use your designs for social media posts, website graphics, printed materials, and more.

Unlock Premium Features: Over offers a free version with limited features, but also offers a premium subscription that unlocks additional templates, fonts, graphics, and other premium features. With a premium subscription, you can access even more creative tools and resources to take your designs to the next level.

Whether you're a social media guru, a small business owner, or just someone who loves creating visual content on the go, Over is a versatile and powerful mobile app that lets you bring your creative visions to life with ease. So, grab your phone, download Over, and let your creativity soar! 📱✨🎨

Procreate

Calling all you artsy book lovers! If you're into hand-drawn illustrations and digital painting, Procreate is the tool for you. It's like having a virtual art studio where you can create custom illustrations for your book that will make your readers swoon. It's the ultimate canvas for your creative genius!

Procreate, the digital canvas for your creative masterpieces! Procreate is a popular digital painting app for artists, illustrators, and creatives that allows you to create stunning digital artwork on your iPad. Here's what makes Procreate a go-to tool for digital artists:

Powerful Brush Engine: Procreate boasts a robust brush engine that offers a wide range of brushes, from realistic brushes that mimic traditional media like pencils, charcoal, and watercolors, to digital brushes for creating unique and stylized effects. The brush engine is highly customizable, allowing you to adjust settings like opacity, flow, size, and more, to achieve the desired look and feel for your artwork.

Intuitive User Interface: Procreate features a user-friendly interface designed for creatives. The app's intuitive layout and gesture-based controls make it easy to navigate and access tools and features, allowing you to focus on your creative process without getting bogged down by complicated menus.

High-Quality Canvas and Resolution: Procreate provides a high-resolution canvas that supports up to 16k by 4k resolution, allowing you to create detailed and high-quality artwork suitable for print or digital media. The app also offers a wide range of canvas sizes and presets, giving you the flexibility to create artwork for various purposes and platforms.

Comprehensive Layering System: Procreate's layering system is powerful and versatile, allowing you to work with multiple layers, adjust their opacity, blending modes, and more. This enables you to create complex and multi-layered artwork with ease, making it a valuable tool for digital painting, illustration, and design.

Extensive Color Tools: Procreate offers a wide range of color tools, including a color picker, color harmony, and color adjustment options, giving you full control over your artwork's color palette. You can create custom color swatches, experiment with different color combinations, and achieve the perfect color balance for your artwork.

Animation Features: Procreate also includes basic animation features, allowing you to create simple animations directly within the app. You can create frame-by-frame animations or use the automatic animation assist to create smooth and dynamic animations, making it a versatile tool for creating animated artwork or gifs.

Seamless Workflow and Export Options: Procreate supports a seamless workflow, allowing you to import and export artwork in various file formats, such as PSD, JPEG, PNG, and more. You can easily export your artwork for print, web, or social media, and share your creations with others or transfer them to other devices for further editing.

Regular Updates and Community Support: Procreate has a vibrant community of artists and creators, and the developers regularly release updates with new features, performance improvements, and bug fixes. The Procreate community is also a valuable resource for learning, sharing tips and tricks, and getting inspired by other artists' work.

Procreate is a powerful and versatile digital painting app that has gained popularity among artists and creatives for its extensive features, intuitive user interface, and high-quality output. Whether you're a professional artist, hobbyist, or just starting out with digital art, Procreate offers a wide range of tools and capabilities to bring your creative visions to life on your iPad. So, grab your Apple Pencil, fire up Procreate, and let your imagination run wild! 🎨 ✨ 🖌

CanBook

It's like a magic wand for book designers. CanBook is an online tool that automates the layout and design process for you. All you have to do is input your content, choose your style, and voila! You'll have a beautifully designed book in minutes. It's like having a design genie grant your book design wishes!

CanBook is an innovative online platform for self-publishing authors that offers a wide range of features to help bring your book to life. Here's a glimpse of what CanBook can do:

Book Formatting: CanBook allows you to easily format your manuscript into a professional-looking book, complete with customizable fonts, spacing, and margins. You can upload your manuscript in various file formats, such as Word or PDF, and CanBook will automatically convert it into an e-book or print-ready PDF.

Cover Design: CanBook provides tools for creating custom book covers, including pre-designed templates or the option to upload your own cover design. You can customize the cover with text, images, and graphics to create an eye-catching cover that reflects your book's genre and style.

Distribution: CanBook offers distribution options that allow you to sell your book through various online retailers, such as Amazon, Barnes & Noble, and more. You can choose to sell your book in e-book format, print-on-demand, or both, giving you flexibility in how you want to reach your readers.

Marketing Tools: CanBook provides marketing tools to help you promote your book, including the ability to create author websites, landing pages, and promotional materials. You can also track sales and royalties, run promotional campaigns, and manage your book's metadata to improve its visibility in online searches.

Author Support: CanBook offers support and resources for self-publishing authors, including tutorials, guides, and a customer support team to assist with any questions or issues you may encounter along the way.

You can also access a community of fellow authors for networking, feedback, and support.

Print-on-Demand: CanBook offers print-on-demand services, allowing you to print physical copies of your book as readers place orders. This eliminates the need for upfront printing costs and inventory management, making it a cost-effective way to offer paperback or hardcover versions of your book.

Royalties and Pricing Control: CanBook provides control over pricing and royalties, allowing you to set your book's price and determine the royalty rates you want to earn. You can adjust prices and royalties at any time, giving you flexibility in pricing strategies and maximizing your earnings.

CanBook offers a comprehensive platform for self-publishing authors, providing a range of features and tools to simplify the publishing process and help you bring your book to market. Whether you're a first-time author or an experienced self-publisher, CanBook offers a user-friendly platform to make your self-publishing journey a success. So, get ready to unleash your creativity, publish your book, and share your story with the world!

BookBrush

If you're all about that book marketing game, BookBrush is the tool for you. It's specifically designed for authors and lets you create eye-catching graphics for your book promotions, social media posts, and ads. It's like having a personal book marketing guru at your fingertips, helping you slay the book design and marketing game.

BookBrush is a versatile online design tool specifically designed for authors and book marketers. With BookBrush, you can create stunning book covers, promotional graphics, and social media posts that are sure to grab attention. The platform offers a wide range of pre-designed templates, fonts, images, and graphics that are specifically tailored for book promotion, making it easy to create eye-catching visuals even if you're not a design pro.

One of the key features of BookBrush is its user-friendly interface that makes designing easy and accessible for authors of all levels of design expertise. You can customize your designs with your own images, book covers, and text, and even add special effects to make your graphics stand out. With BookBrush, you can create promotional materials that are optimized for various social media platforms, including Facebook, Instagram, Twitter, and more, helping you effectively promote your book to your target audience.

BookBrush also offers a range of additional features, such as the ability to create 3D book mockups, animated book covers, and even book trailers. You can also schedule and automate your social media posts directly from BookBrush, making it a convenient all-in-one tool for your book promotion needs. Whether you're a new author looking to create professional book graphics or a seasoned book marketer seeking to streamline your promotional efforts, BookBrush is a powerful and user-friendly tool that can help you create visually stunning graphics to promote your book and engage with readers. So, get ready to brush up on your book marketing game with BookBrush!

DIY

Last but not least, the ultimate book design tool - your creativity and resourcefulness! With a little DIY spirit, you can create unique and personalized book layouts using a combination of free design tools, clipart, and your own artistic flair. It's like a DIY craft project, but for book design. So grab your laptop, put on your creative hat, and let your imagination run wild!

DIY allow authors and self-publishers to design and format their books independently, without the need for professional design services. These programs typically offer user-friendly interfaces and pre-designed templates that make it easy for authors to create their own book layouts, add images, adjust text formatting, and customize the overall design of their books.

One of the key advantages of using a DIY book layout program is the cost-effectiveness. Hiring a professional designer for book layout can be expensive, especially for self-published authors on a budget. DIY book layout programs provide a more affordable option for authors who want to take control of their book's design process and save on design costs. Additionally, DIY book layout programs often offer flexibility and creative freedom, allowing authors to express their unique vision and style through their book's design.

However, it's important to note that DIY book layout programs may have limitations compared to professional design services. They may not offer the same level of customization, advanced features, or access to high-quality design elements as professional design tools. Additionally, authors may need to invest time and effort into learning how to use the software effectively. Overall, DIY book layout programs can be a great option for authors who are willing to put in the effort to learn and create their own book layouts, but it's important to weigh the pros and cons and choose a program that best fits your specific needs and design goals. Happy designing! 📑 ✨ ✏️

(((((((((o)))))))))

So there you have it, my fellow book-loving friends. Whether you're an aspiring author, a self-publisher, or just a book nerd who loves playing with design tools, these programs are here to help you bring your book to life in a fun and stylish way. Happy designing, and may your book be the talk of the town!

You want some more?

Yo, you've got it! We've got you covered with more dopest software to design and format your book like a boss. Check it out:

LitLayout Pro: This app is lit AF when it comes to designing your book. With drag-and-drop features and customizable templates, you can create a lit book cover and format the pages like a pro. It's so easy to use, even your grandma could do it.

WordWizard Pro: This software is a word nerd's dream come true. It's got all the dope tools to help you format your book like a champ. From setting margins to adding footnotes, WordWizard Pro makes it a breeze to create a book that's straight fire.

CoverCrusher: Need a killer book cover that will make your readers go "wow"? Look no further than CoverCrusher. This app has a lit collection of pre-designed covers that you can customize to match your vibe. Say goodbye to basic covers and hello to cover goals!

FontFreak: Fonts matter, peeps! With FontFreak, you can get your typography game on point. Choose from a wide range of rad fonts that will make your book look fresh and unique. You'll be the envy of all the book nerds in town.

ProsePolisher: Don't let grammar mistakes cramp your style. ProsePolisher is the ultimate writing tool that will help you catch those sneaky typos and grammatical errors. It's like having your own personal grammar guru, and it's a must-have for any aspiring author.

Putting the 'Fun' in Publishing Fundamentals

So, there you have it, fellow authors! Hopefully our nuggets of tips, guides and advices will help you in your journey to publish your book.

No more struggling with formatting issues or feeling lost in the publishing process – our guides and support are here to empower you every step of the way. From unleashing your creativity to ensuring your book shines with professionalism, we've got your back.

So, dive into the world of self-publishing with confidence, knowing that you have our guidance and assistance to rely on. Let your book soar to new heights, captivate readers, and leave a lasting impression. We're here to help you make your publishing dreams a reality.

Happy writing, my fellow wordsmiths! May your literary adventure be filled with endless possibilities, unrivaled satisfaction, and a book that shines as brightly as a supernova in the vast galaxy of literature. You've got this!